URBAN ANDES

DESIGN-LED EXPLORATIONS TO TACKLE
CLIMATE CHANGE

LEUVEN UNIVERSITY
PRESS

EDITED BY
VIVIANA D'AURIA,
WARD VERBAKEL,
BASIL DESCHEEMAEKER

LAP

The peer-reviewed series LAP *(Landscape and Architecture Projections)* focuses on design research in the fields of architecture, urbanism and landscape. It seeks to highlight innovative practices worldwide which boldly address the most pressing socio-political, ecological and spatial issues of the contemporary times. It emphasizes work which is developed in cooperation with activists and civil society, various governmental and/or development agencies and stakeholders as well as with other experts.

Series Editors
    Kelly Shannon
    Ward Verbakel

Editorial Board
    Eliana Barbosa
    Margarita Jover Biboum
    Ilze Wolff

FOREWORD

This publication launches LAP, a new series on landscape and architecture design research. From a theoretical as well as an applied perspective, design-led research has the potential to contribute to both international academic discourse and the tacit knowledge embedded in localized transformation practices. The intrinsic nature of the design field to revisit, recombine, and reformulate disparate pieces of knowledge in a circular, not always linear manner is part of this LAP series' DNA. Consequently, it explicitly uses visual components as an important and essential foil to textual insights. Through this series we pursue a diversity of design and research practices that occur beyond mainstream sites, assignments, and programmes. Here, as demonstrated in this first issue, the emphasis will fall on design-led research developed in cooperation with civil society, local and international stakeholders, governmental and non-governmental agencies and several experts.

The idea of urbanity is linked to the Andes in the collective imagination, primarily through the iconic image of Machu Picchu as seen from the top of adjacent Huayna Picchu: an abandoned Inca city, perched on a mountaintop, under siege from the surrounding nature. The claim of LAP 01 for the present-day Andes as urban–and to claim this urbanity not as a smattering of isolated exceptions but as a condition that permeates large portions of the region–is to challenge this all too picturesque notion and to acknowledge existing and long-standing regional realities. Conversely, to attach the attributive 'Andean' to the concept of urbanism raises a different set of questions. How do cities develop in a context so hostile to concentrated human presence? What manipulations of the land are required? What form might a sustainable urbanism in the Andes adopt, and how can this urbanism engage with the existing and future effects of climate change?

The texts and design research projects collected here focus on a specific Peruvian case: the catchment of the Cachi River and its main city, Ayacucho. The work does not attempt to formulate a 'unifying theoretical framework' for the Urban Andes, and the case study does not claim to represent urbanization in and of the Andes at large. Rather, the aim is that these design-led and site-specific reflections serve as an introduction. For an audience from the Global North: to a portion of the Andes, through one example of its settlement, and to a set of indigenous practices and their potential to formulate answers to contemporary challenges of climate change. For an Andean audience: to pay homage to landscape urbanism and design methods which may (or may not) be new to them.

On the one hand, it is a synthesis of the knowledge and design strategies collected and developed through a research project called 'Urban Andes', initiated by the KU Leuven Faculty of Engineering Sciences' Department of Architecture, the *Centro de Competencias del Agua*, and their partners in 2018-2020. That collaboration consisted of several exchanges (workshops, debate, seminars, lectures, and research) along with extensive fieldwork and stakeholder interaction. This synthesis reconsiders and reconfigures the heterogenous pieces of information and knowledge acquired. It gains coherence through several narratives that include design research, interpretative mapping, and hypothetical strategies for future territorial transformations. On the other hand, this publication is premised on the hope of it forming one of the bases for next steps: a re-expansion of this compressed essence towards new lines of research, additional design proposals, new collaborations, local interventions, and engagement with other Andean contexts.

The first part of the LAP 01 publication draws up the *frame* in which this collaboration and research takes place. It unpacks a broader investigation of the particularities of urban and landscape practices in the context of the Andes and their challenges in a changing environment. The interdependency of the Cachi Basin and the city of Ayacucho is explored both as a theoretical discourse and as a set of parallel narratives in which image and word merge into a graphical essay. The second half of this publication looks ahead through a *projection* constructed from a multitude of design strategies, workshop concepts, and a shared discourse on future directions.

   Basil Descheemaeker,
   Ward Verbakel

(RE)FRAMING THE URBAN ANDES

MARGARITA MACERA CARNERO
& MONICA RIVERA MUÑOZ

Andean urbanism, a co-evolution of landscape and settlement(s)

Contemporary Andean cities like Ayacucho appear to be a paradox (Makowski, 2008). Since the fifteenth century, intermontane valley sites were not places of human agglomeration–nor were they sites of permanent occupation–but rather administrative and ceremonial locales as well as resting areas for armies passing through (Mumford, 2012; Tello, 1921, 1942). Low-valley settlements were merely part of broader and diffused networks of self-subsistence that sustained agro-pastoral economies. For a long time, Andean 'urbanism' relied upon resilient agro-pastoral regimes that adapted to cyclic variations in climate and the rise or collapse of pan-Andean states. Andean cities –as we know them today–are on the other hand detached from these enduring regimes that were embedded in the landscape. Established during the Spanish regime (1532–1821) with no consideration for pre-existing settlement patterns, 'cities' served as colonial outposts for the (limited) Spanish colonial elite–in addition to government, market, and church institutions. In the twenty-first century, as a result, Andean cities like Ayacucho have had to synchronize their development with the long-term socio-ecological dynamics that preceded their making. In the face of global climate change, and particularly in water-scarce contexts and semi-arid regions like Ayacucho, Andean resilience urgently calls for a re-articulation of urbanization and its position within broader landscape dynamics.

In terms of water shortage, notable precedents of Andean resilience during drought date back to the twelfth century. Not by chance, a period of regional drought coincided with the collapse of the pan-Andean states of Wari and Tiahuanaco–with Ayacucho (Peru) and La Paz (Bolivia) as their respective capital cities (Macera, 1978; Tello, 1929, 1942). To overcome water scarcity, agricultural activities shifted from low-valley maize agriculture to tuber cultivation in the highlands, which could bear lower temperatures, frosts, and water scarcity. By adapting to changes in production regimes, large populations migrated to higher altitudes (between 3.500 and 4.200 meters), in addition to these new crops (Kellet, 2010). At the same time, highland migration facilitated access to pastoral and water resources from adjacent headwater areas. Competition over resources led to the construction of neighbourhoods on mountain peaks, where panoramic views allowed for the maintenance of defensive positions. By the time the Incan state surged to prominence in the mid-fifteenth century, hilltop and mountain-slope settlements predominated, located adjacent to scant pockets of fertile land, be these natural or artificial. Alongside drastic changes in land production systems, such a settlement location strategy allowed Andean populations to thrive despite stark environmental challenges.

In Ayacucho, known as Huamanga during the Incan empire, Andean communities established social and landscape systems to overcome overall scarcity. By necessity, solidarity among members of same ethnic groups led to mechanisms of production and redistribution of goods based on reciprocity, not to mention across ecological floors (Murra, 1972; Pulgar Vidal, 1946)). Significant differences in microclimates across short vertical distances (Tosi, 1960) enabled dispersed communities to specialize in the production of certain crops and goods. Mechanisms of exchange allowed these communities to pool resources and consequently have access to otherwise unattainable products. Accordingly, settlement patterns and productive systems stretched from highland plateaus to coastal plains and rainforest valleys. In headwater areas (above 3.500 meters altitude), networks of constructed *qochas* (rain-fed water catchments) and afforestation practices (mainly of *polylepis*) increased water retention (Tello, 1942). Extensive canal systems made it possible to transport water to massively constructed *andenes* (agro-pastoral terraces) located on mountain slopes situated below 3.500 meters. Such comprehensive manipulation of the landscape (earth, water, vegetation) was exactly what guaranteed the system's water and food security as well as livestock movements between floors on uncultivated lands.

Until the end of the fifteenth century, Andean settlements co-evolved with dynamic practices of water, livestock, and agriculture management, though also with relentless montane deforestation. Sustained food security triggered demographic growth which in turn prompted more settlement construction. As new neighbourhoods colonized further fertile niches, steady deforestation incited widespread soil erosion as well as loss of nutrients in mountain slopes. Subsequent Spanish colonization (1535-1821) would accelerate deforestation practices that pre-dated their conquest of indigenous territory (Lynch, 1990). Related extractive procedures, such as the mining of silver, demanded large volumes of wood for use as construction materials and fuel (Robins, 2011). Between 1550 and 1580, the forced resettlement of indigenous populations to colonial redoubts led to the abandonment of many productive niches traditionally dispersed across different ecological floors. Productive sites were then reclaimed by Spanish landlords. In the absence of communities, spontaneous, bushy vegetation started to grow on unclaimed sites (Ansión, 1986). Not long after forced resettlement, satellite communities began to commandeer new and old niches around novel concentrations of human agglomeration: colonial mines and cities. A new constellation of settlements was formed while removing the emergent vegetation. Along with disrupting territorial indigenous organization, the Spanish conquered and re-founded settlement networks, as well as consolidated colonial expansion in the Americas in ecologically violent ways. Colonial oppression materialized in the design of a binary landscape model that assigned valleys to the colonizers, while indigenous populations were pushed towards sterile lands and mountains (Rivera Muñoz, 2019). Termed the valley-upland model (Zimmerer & Bell, 2015), this landscape model developed during the sixteenth and seventeenth centuries, and it describes the introduction of a "binary and relational territorial logic of settled/unsettled" (Zimmerer & Bell, 2015, p. 104). Valley areas were highly valued for their fertility, high productivity for Spanish food goods, and regarded as 'healthy locations'. Cities were founded there on top of pre-existing settlements and acquired the quality of fixed spaces of colonial order. By contrast, the higher lands were seen as barren and desolate and became looser spaces, less subject to Spanish control, more isolated, though where rural settlements also (re)appeared. The dominance of the binary distinction in apprehending the territory had important effects on the socio-ecological interactions therein. Thenceforth, valley and upland, formerly complementary spaces, were projected as centre and periphery. This ideological and spatial disruption is an evident and dismal legacy still recognizable in most Andean territories, where valleys (and cities) persist as places of concentration–the poles of economic and political power–while upland territories have become subordinated landscapes, where people and natural resources can be extracted and are at the service of cities (Macera, 2020).

Over time, the persistent interpretation of the landscape as two distinct areas (valley/upland) has rendered other disjunctions, especially in terms of socio-ecological challenges. Power differences between valley and upland populations, socio-economic inequalities, imbalances between the extraction of resources versus limited public investment in social, conservation, and infrastructure programs in upland territories, among others, are all a direct result of the binary distinctions embedded in colonial rule. This pervasive legacy also works to the detriment of rural landscapes and of those who inhabit them, which moreover results in: lack of opportunity (especially for the youth); abandonment of agricultural practices, which in turn threatens food security; persistent rural out-migration; and consequent intensification of urbanization in the valleys.

After Peruvian independence in 1821, large estate landlords (mainly of Spanish descent) inherited and monopolized the most productive plots of land for extensive commercial agriculture. By consequence, remaining mountain slopes now managed by Andean landholders can hardly be but over-exploited, deepening rural poverty and triggering massive migration towards cities (Matos Mar, 1986). Although the 1969 land reform allowed for the redistribution of land among local communities, it failed to solve the lack of financial capital required to upkeep large *haciendas* (Eguren, 2006). Rural poverty and rapid urbanization continued, nevertheless. By 1980, these intertwined processes kick-started the *Sendero Luminoso* (Shining Path) and the beginning of a twelve-year-long armed conflict, with Ayacucho as its epicentre. Sendero's attacks on Andean communities–and the counteroffensive by the Peruvian army–induced the massive flight of rural communities towards cities. Between 1980 and 1992, Ayacucho's urban population grew by more than 60 percent (*Instituto Nacional de Estadística e Informática* [INEI], 2017). Rapid urbanization–namely, in the form of land annexations–occurred in all directions of the valley regardless of pre-existing vegetation, difficult topography, and lack of sufficient water provision. Ayacucho's accelerated urbanization was therefore accompanied by intense landscape degradation, that is, deforestation, erosion, and consequent loss of the land's water regulation capacity. Hosting more than three times the population it had in 1960 (INEI, 2017), today Ayacucho's urban growth continues to challenge the capacity of local ecologies for supporting demographic pressure. New ecological changes further challenge the possibility for cities such as Ayacucho to achieve overall resilience, particularly in relation to water security. Current challenges include addressing the effects of global climate change in Andean headwater sources that are vital for local ecosystems as well as for rural and urban water provision at lower ecological floors.

Climate change and current challenges to urbanization in the Andes

Climate change is altering water cycles and water availability in cities. The issue is especially pressing for mountain settlements, like those located in the semi-arid Andes, where water resources are partially dependent on high-altitude glaciers. The combined effects of climate change (rising temperatures, drastic glacier shrinkage, and rainfall variability and unpredictability) are markedly affecting the reliability of water resources and radically changing water provision patterns. Mountains are the "world's natural water towers" (Ragettli et al., 2016; p. 9222), even though mountain regions are expected to experience the strongest effects of global warming, especially in places located south of latitude 11° south (Buytaert & De Bièvre, 2012). The combination of a precipitation decrease and temperature increase will likely raise evapotranspiration values, thus reducing overall water availability for human settlements and heavily impacting the social and economic development of populations in mountainous regions.

These changes are not only of natural origin but are also induced by human populations (Van Loon et al., 2016). Buytaert and De Bièvre (2012) argue that the impact of population growth may be more determinant for urban water supplies than the effects of climate change are (Buytaert & De Bièvre, 2012; Buytaert et al., 2006). Water resources, however, are ever more difficult to ensure. Ayacucho faces the tangible effects of both demographic growth and climate change. Located in the headwaters of the Cachi Basin, Ayacucho's high-altitude glaciers have been primary sources for urban and rural water provision. Due to their melting, the Cachi's rural and urban communities are in fierce competition over access to water. To confront the effects of climate change on water availability, it becomes urgent to deal in a more integrated manner with soil and water management, biodiversity conservation, and urbanism–not to mention taking actions to treat and plan the socio-environmental connectivity between upper and lower basins. This means that such actions need to include populations' well-being, in which Andean social structures and mechanisms of reciprocity are integrated into tailored processes towards building capacity for local communities.

Some organizations are leading research and actions in this regard. To increase water retention, highland communities–in collaboration with local NGO CEDAP (*Centro de Desarrollo Agropecuario* [Centre of Agricultural and Livestock Development])–have returned to and renewed pre-colonial water management strategies, such as the construction of *qochas* and afforestation of *polylepis* in headwater areas. From the highlands, new networks of *qochas* aim to harvest rainfall for local communities while enhancing overall water security in the basin. These works on landscape manipulation are complemented by a more long-term effort towards building competencies, as developed by CEDAP in tandem with the local population. Training of young leaders, women's empowerment, and strengthening of landscape planning skills are among the capacities under development. Unfortunately, such efforts are insufficient if the linear consumption of landscape resources unwaveringly continues in the urban lowlands. Nonetheless, CEDAP's attention for adapting water management projects in rural highlands to the urban condition has been fundamental–not only for the articulation of the Urban Andes project, but also in showing the way forward in revising water-based practices in Ayacucho and its region.

For effectively tackling the contradictions posed by overconsumption in a water-scarce territory, it becomes urgent to develop strategies that can further integrate different resources, traditions, and technologies across urban and rural domains. This approach diverges from conventional top-down practices of water management by way of grey infrastructure construction, as exemplified by the hydraulic syphons and concrete canals realized in Ayacucho. Besides high costs and limited adaptive capacity (Ochoa-Tocachi et al., 2019), these infrastructures very often have negative impacts on ecosystems and ultimately also on local livelihoods (Palmer et al., 2015). Alternatively, as the work of CEDAP illustrates, new landscape infrastructures can learn from traditional local practices which have demonstrated efficiency in the articulation of settlement resilience. Ancient Andean practices have the potential to inform current responses to climate change impacts in Ayacucho and other Andean regions.

> Andean Urbanism renewed:
> landscape strategies for resilient
> cities in the Urban Andes

(Re)-framing Andean urbanism necessarily entails understanding the evolution of broader settlement and landscape systems, both in time and space. Re-establishing a water balance in the Cachi Basin therefore requires a profound acknowledgement of how urban and rural ecologies are interconnected in terms of water management. Circumscribed within the Cachi Basin, the city of Ayacucho needs to recalibrate its water management mechanisms within broader water needs extending beyond its urban confines. In the face of urbanization, unsustainable practices, and climate change, new strategies for landscape urbanism are urgently needed in order to counter water scarcity. In this context, the Urban Andes initiative tackles the issue of water insecurity and unsustainable urbanization by foregrounding Andean livelihoods, in addition to considering the city of Ayacucho and the semi-arid Cachi Basin as instructive cases of an urban/rural water balance that has reached a tipping point. Relying on landscape urbanism, the Urban Andes project addresses Ayacucho's water insecurity at multiple scales. The domestic scale is touched upon both in the city itself and in the context of peripheral urban tissues. These are articulated by considering the larger landscape systems, that is, sub-catchments of the Cachi Basin, from the headwaters to the floodplains. Starting from the idea that pre-colonial water practices further away in the headwaters –and their re-articulation by communities and organizations such as CEDAP–is exemplary, the study that follows suggests future strategies for the missing pieces downstream, while taking inspiration from nature-based solutions in the meantime.

Long-standing practices that have constructed the Andean landscape over time have therefore inspired the design investigations presented in this booklet, which can hopefully inform local urban planning and sustain self-organized practices in emerging districts. Design-based research has led to the identification of key interventions for Ayacucho's landscape reconfiguration (land cover, topography, etc.) and for the development of new urban typologies (public space, housing, and social infrastructure) to improve overall water management practices and favour water retention. Increasing on-site water catchment can in fact reduce pressure on water sources from distant headwater areas, thus enhancing self-sustainable and cyclic processes of urban water management.

By building on lessons from indigenous landscape management practices of the Peruvian Andes, the Urban Andes initiative promotes the use of low-tech, integrated, and sophisticated design solutions for water management. Accumulated knowledge embedded in vernacular techniques, using locally available materials, reduces dependence on external interventions and does not require costly investments. The re-articulation of indigenous water management practices may benefit from existing forms of social organization for the self-provision of infrastructure. They are capable of simultaneously addressing the pressing issues of water scarcity as well as improving public space and infrastructure, especially within urban and rural communities where public investment lags far behind.

As an international and inter-institutional initiative, our Urban Andes project has brought together local academic and public institutions, as well as international academic and non-governmental entities. By means of intensive design-based workshops, proposals at various scales were developed by interdisciplinary groups of practitioners, policy makers, local actors, and authorities. Seminars and related events have opened space for the development of research by both local and international young practitioners and graduate students in Ayacucho, supporting further dissemination of the project's main investigations and findings. While paying homage to indigenous practices of water management, Urban Andes has aimed to influence the *modus operandi* of several stakeholders active in Ayacucho. Partnerships with a community of practitioners, researchers, and designers in search of methods for repairing the Andean territory have been essential. The propositions raised by the project are seen as a framework that can support initial steps for the territory's transformation as a way forward for the sustainable growth and water security of other settlements in the Andean region.

References

Ansión, J. (1986). *El árbol y el bosque en la sociedad Andina* [The tree and the forest in Andean society]. Lima: FAO.

Buytaert, W, & De Bièvre, B. (2012). Water for cities: The impact of climate change and demographic growth in the tropical Andes. *Water Resources Research, 48,* 8, 1–13.

Buytaert, Wouter, Célleri, R., De Bièvre, B., Cisneros, F., Wyseure, G., Deckers, J., & Hofstede, R. (2006). Human impact on the hydrology of the Andean páramos. *Earth-Science Reviews, 79,* 1–2, 53–72.

Eguren, F. (2006). Reforma agraria y desarrollo rural en el Perú [Land reform and rural development in Peru]. In *Reforma agraria y desarrollo rural en la región andina* [Land reform and rural development in the Andean region] (pp. 11–31). Lima: Centro Peruano de Estudios Sociales.

Instituto Nacional de Estadística e Informática. (2017). *Evolución de la población censada urbana, según departamento, 1940, 1961, 1972, 1981, 1993, 2007 y 2017* [Evolution of the registered urban population, by department, 1940, 1961, 1972, 1981, 1993, 2007 and 2017]. Retrieved from https://www.inei.gob.pe/estadisticas/indice-tematico/poblacion-y-vivienda/

Kellet, L. (2010). *Chanka settlement ecology: Hilltop sites, land use and warfare in late prehispanic Andahuaylas, Peru* [Unpublished doctoral dissertation]. University of New Mexico.

Loon, A. F. V., Stahl, K., Baldassarre, G. D., Clark, J., Rangecroft, S., Wanders, N., Gleeson, T., Dijk, A. I. J. M. V., Tallaksen, L. M., Hannaford, J., Uijlenhoet, R., Teuling, A. J., Hannah, D. M., Sheffield, J., Svoboda, M., Verbeiren, B., Wagener, T., & Lanen, H. A. J. V. (2016). Drought in a human-modified world: Reframing drought definitions, understanding, and analysis approaches. *Hydrology and Earth System Sciences, 20,* 9, 3631–3650. https://doi.org/10.5194/hess-20-3631-2016

Lynch, T. F. (1990). Quaternary climate, environment, and the human occupation of the south-central Andes. *Geoarchaeology, 5,* 3, 199–228.

Macera, M. (2020). *Anticipating the post-mining landscapes of Cajamarca, North Andes of Peru. The agency of mining (closure)* [Unpublished doctoral dissertation]. KU Leuven.

Macera, P. (1978). *Visión histórica del Perú (del Paleolítico al proceso de 1968)* [Historical vision of Peru from the Paleolithic to the 1968 process]. Lima: Editorial Milla Batres.

Makowski, K. (2008). Andean Urbanism. In *The handbook of South American archaeology* (pp. 633–657). New York: Springer.

Matos Mar, J. (1986). *Desborde popular y crisis del Estado. El nuevo rostro del Perú en la década de 1980* [Popular overflow and crisis of the State. The new face of Peru in the 1980s]. Lima: Instituto de Estudios Peruanos.

Mumford, J. R. (2012). *Vertical Empire. The general resettlement of Indians in the colonial Andes.* Durham, NC, and London: Duke University Press.

Murra, J. (1972). *El 'control vertical' de un máximo de pisos ecológicos en la economía de las sociedades Andinas* ['Vertical control' of a maximum of ecological floors in the economy of Andean societies]. Huánuco: Universidad Nacional Hermilio Vardizán.

Ochoa-Tocachi, B. F., Bardales, J. D., Antiporta, J., Pérez, K., Acosta, L., Mao, F., Zulkafli, Z., Gil-Ríos, J., Angulo, O., Grainger, S., Gammie, G., De Bièvre, B., & Buytaert, W. (2019). Potential contributions of pre-Inca infiltration infrastructure to Andean water security. *Nature Sustainability, 2,* 7, 584–593. https://doi.org/10.1038/s41893-019-0307-1

Palmer, M. A., Liu, J., Matthews, J. H., Mumba, M., & D'Odorico, P. (2015). WATER. Manage water in a green way. *Science (New York, N.Y.), 349,* 6248, 584–585. https://doi.org/10.1126/science.aac7778

Pulgar Vidal, J. (1946). *Historia y geografía del Perú: Las ocho regiones naturales del Perú* [History and geography of Peru: The eight natural regions of Peru] (1st ed.). Lima: Universidad Nacional Mayor de San Marcos.

Ragettli, S., Immerzeel, W. W., & Pellicciotti, F. (2016). Contrasting climate change impact on river flows from high-altitude catchments in the Himalayan and Andes Mountains. *Proceedings of the National Academy of Sciences, 113,* 33, 9222–9227. https://doi.org/10.1073/pnas.1606526113

Rivera, M. M. (2019). *Landscapes in-between. Highlands urbanization and resistance in the Andes (Cuenca, Ecuador)* [Unpublished doctoral dissertation]. KU Leuven.

Robins, N.A. (2011). *Mercury, mining, and empire. The human and ecological costs of colonial silver mining in the Andes.* Bloomington, IN: Indiana University Press

Tello, J. C. (1921). *Introducción a la historia antigua del Perú* [Introduction to ancient history of Peru]. Lima: Editorial Euforion.

Tello, J. C. (1929). *Antiguo Perú: primera época* [Ancient Peru: first epoch]. Lima: Comisión Organizadora del Segundo Congreso Sudamericano de Turismo.

Tello, J. C. (1942). *Origen y desarrollo de las civilizaciones prehistóricas andinas.* Lima: Librería e imprenta Gil.

Tosi, J. A. (1960). *Zonas de vida natural en el Perú: memoria explicativa sobre el mapa ecológico del Perú: Memoria explicativa sobre el mapa ecológico del Perú* [Natural life zones in Peru: Explanatory memory of the ecological map of Peru] (Vol. 5). Lima: Instituto Interamericano de Ciencias Agrícolas de la OEA, Zona Andina.

Zimmerer, K. S., & Bell, M. G. (2015). Time for change: The legacy of a Euro-Andean model of landscape versus the need for landscape connectivity. *Landscape and Urban Planning, 139,* 104–116. https://doi.org/10.1016/j.landurbplan.2015.02.002

PARALLEL NARRATIVES FOR CITY AND BASIN

BASIL DESCHEEMAEKER, WARD VERBAKEL,
LOUISE BLANCQUAERT, ELISABETH DE CLERCQ,
THOMAS HAWER, WILLEM HUBRECHTS,
SIGRID VANGENEUGDEN, VIVIANA D'AURIA

The interrelationships between the ecology and landscape of the Cachi River basin and its indigenous, colonial, and post-colonial inhabitation cannot be contained in any one story. Instead of attempting to formulate a 'unifying theoretical framework', we frame the topic from three thematic entry points: water, human settlements, and soil. While each thematic part functions as a stand-alone narrative, it is in their parallel reading that the richness of the subject becomes most apparent.[1] The narratives take the form of a graphical essay that combines text and image in one continuous flow.

[1] This triple narrative does not claim to be 'complete' either. The three parallel narratives represent the frame used throughout the Urban Andes project research and design explorations. Other readings and points of view can and should be added to further deepen the understanding of the territory.

[2] The Köppen-Geiger classification for Ayacucho (alt. 2.750 m a.s.l.), the basin's primary city, is BSk or 'cold semi-arid climate'.

[3] CCA, 2017

[4] Drenkhan et al., 2015

[5] Maldonado Fonkén, 2014

I.

THE LIFE FORCE
OF THE MOUNTAINS

A natural hydrology

The Cachi River basin, situated in the sierra or Andean highlands of Peru, is a far-flung portion of the vast Amazon watershed. Its headwaters are found at an altitude of ca. 5.000 m a.s.l., and it flows into the Mantaro River at 2.150 m a.s.l.. The basin's climate is semi-arid,[2] with a long dry season lasting from April to November, and a short wet season. →fig. 1-5

In the highest reaches of the basin, frequent sub-zero temperatures cause this seasonal precipitation to accumulate in the form of snow and glaciers.[3] Additionally, natural lakes–known as *qochas*–retain rain–and meltwater.[4] Throughout the year, the glaciers and *qochas* gradually release their stored water, allowing it to infiltrate into the soil and reappear elsewhere as natural springs (known locally as *ojos de agua* or 'water eyes'. These springs in turn feed the *bofedales:* spongy wetlands located in the upper basin that further slow the downhill flow of water.[5]

fig. 1–2

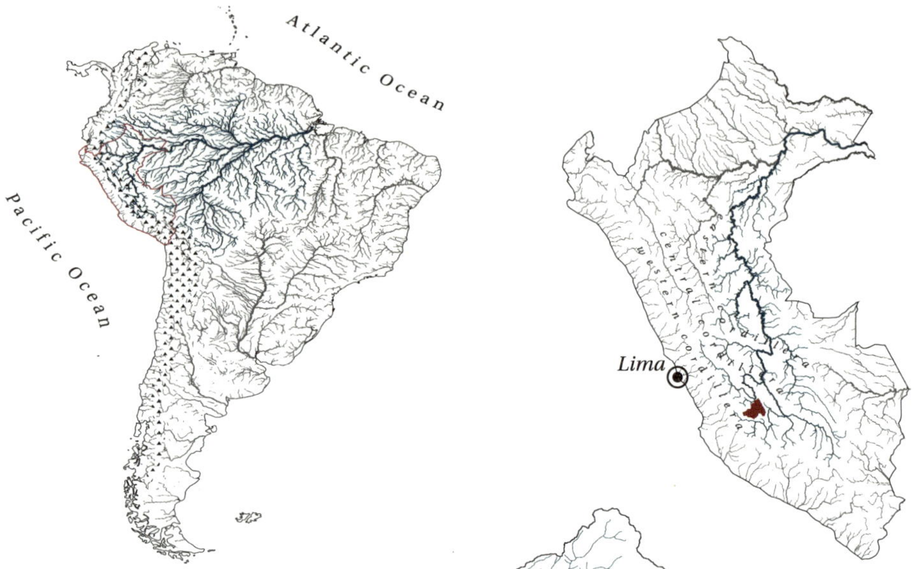

Atlantic Ocean
Pacific Ocean
Lima

fig. 3

fig. 4–5

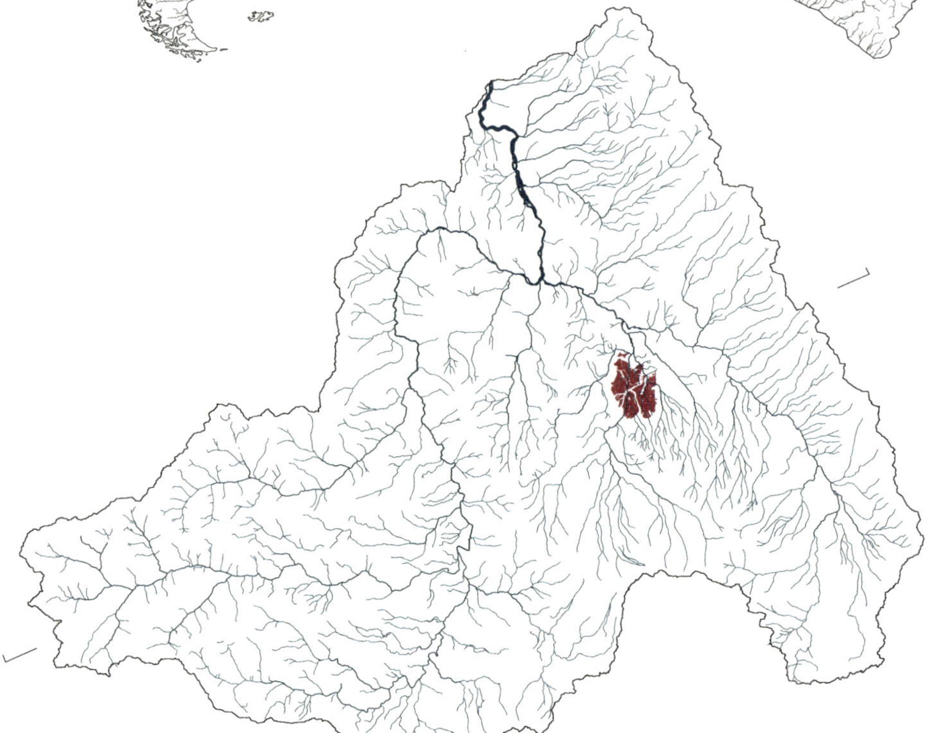

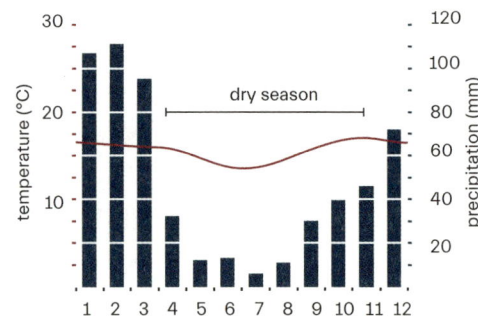

headwaters
Ayacucho
5000 m
2500 m
0
100 km
30
20
10
temperature (°C)
120
100
80
60
40
20
precipitation (mm)
dry season
1 2 3 4 5 6 7 8 9 10 11 12

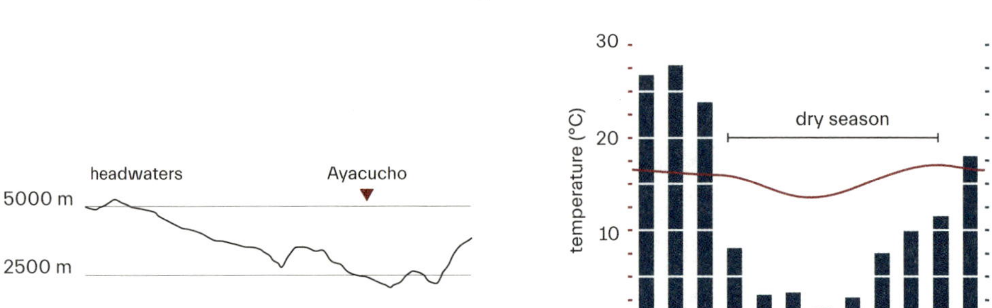

Section of the Cachi River basin

Climatograph of Ayacucho (CCA, 2017)

The combination of glaciers, *qochas* and *bofedales* plays a crucial role in the natural hydrological system of the basin. They form an enormous buffer, providing the areas downstream with a year-round supply of water even during the dry season.

Starting in pre-Incan times, a dispersed structure of smaller settlements has formed that is strongly linked to this hydrological system.[6] The vegetation of the *bofedales* is grazed by livestock–historically camelids such as llamas and alpacas, though currently also cattle and sheep. Where an additional supply of water is required, natural depressions in the terrain are enclosed with small dams, creating artificial lakes that are likewise called *qochas*. From here, the flow of water to adjacent fields can be regulated via simple irrigation systems. This sensitive and measured relationship to water is engrained in the Andean cosmovision, which considers the flow of water to be the 'life force of the mountains'.[7]

6   Lumbreras, 2006, p. 18
7   *La sangre de las montañas* (Miranda Zambrano, Lindo Revilla, Santana Paucar, 2000, p. 213). Although a more precise translation of *sangre* would be 'blood' or 'life-blood', the choice was made to stay away from translations that might (incorrectly) refer to the armed conflict that took place in the region at the end of the 20th century (see further).

However, the traditional balance between water and settlement patterns is currently under pressure on two fronts. Firstly, due to climate change, temperatures in the basin are rising,[8] causing the glaciers to melt. Climate change is also leading to a decrease in annual precipitation and longer periods of drought.[9] Deforestation and erosion result in increased quantity and speed of surface runoff. Consequently, the capacity of the upper basin to buffer water is decreasing. Secondly, strong demographic growth in Ayacucho[10] and Huanta–the basin's primary cities–means water demand is expanding both rapidly and in very concentrated areas, in a manner that is at odds with the capillary, diffuse character of the natural water system.

A less constant supply of water puts the traditional highland communities at risk, forcing them to be increasingly dependent on artificial *qochas* in order to maintain not only their crops but also the grasslands and *bofedales*.

Engineering the basin

For Ayacucho, bypassed by the major natural water flow of the basin, retaining more water from its own microwatershed is not sufficient to satisfy both the increased water demand for domestic use and the wish to augment the surface of irrigated agriculture near to the city. As a result, large, heavily engineered infrastructure projects have been and continue to be constructed that modify the hydrological system on the scale of the basin. →fig. 6–8

The most far-reaching of these is the Cachi River Project, which diverts water from the western watersheds towards the immense[11] Cuchoquesera reservoir, and

---

8   Buytaert, De Bièvre, 2012
9   Drenkhan et al., 2015
10 Between 1993 and 2007, the population of the city of Ayacucho is estimated to have increased from 105.918 to 151.019: an average yearly growth of 2,5% (INEI, 2017, p. 68).
11 The reservoir has an estimated capacity of 80 million litres (GESAAM, 2016, p. 54).

from there to Ayacucho and its adjacent agricultural lands. In doing so, this intervention further imperils highland communities and ecologies by cutting them off from their natural reservoirs in the upper basin.

Despite the extensive investment of resources, continued urban expansion means this system too will soon meet its limits. And when it does, urban water provision will be prioritized over agricultural irrigation,[12] thus posing a risk not only to rural livelihoods but also to the food security of the city itself. For this reason, extensions to the Cachi River Project are already being planned. Still, there is only so much water available in the basin, and the current infrastructural approach will bleed the basin dry. Sooner or later this reality will force action to be taken on the other side of the equation: a more efficient management of water consumption, with a focus on storage and reuse of rain- and wastewater.

[12] Interview with Meza Lazaro, engineer for SEDA (*Servicio de Agua Potable y Alcantarillado de Ayacucho*), 2018

❶ water intake
❷ water reservoir Cuchoquesera
❸ irrigation zone: upper basin
❹ tunnel
❺ irrigation zone: lower basin
❻ irrigation zone: Socos
❼ Ayacucho

river
canal
water intake
dammed reservoir
irrigated area
RESPONSIBLE OPERATOR

MAX WATER FLUX [M³/S]
0.10 —— to Ayacucho
0.50 —— to Socos
0.85 —— to Ayacucho
2.00 —— to upper basin
4.90 —— to lower basin
7.00 —— to tunnel
0.70 —— to Cuchoquesera

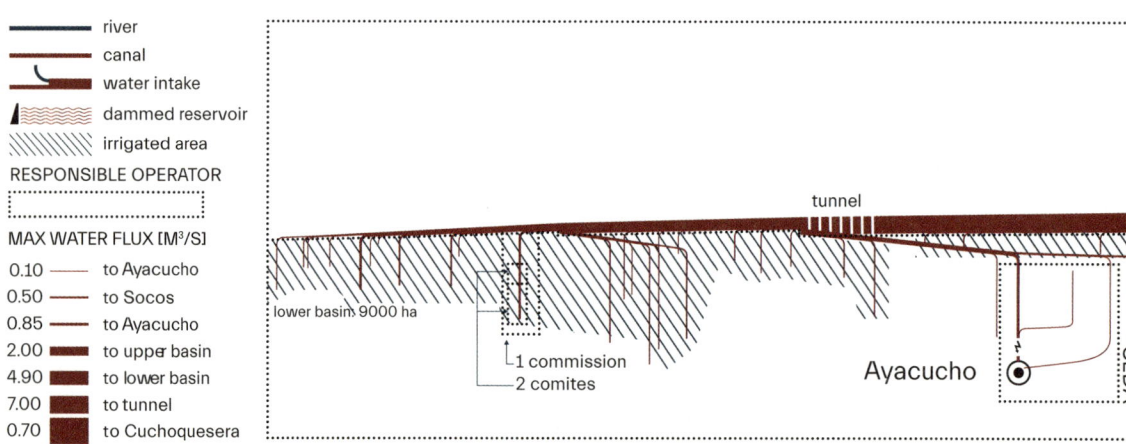

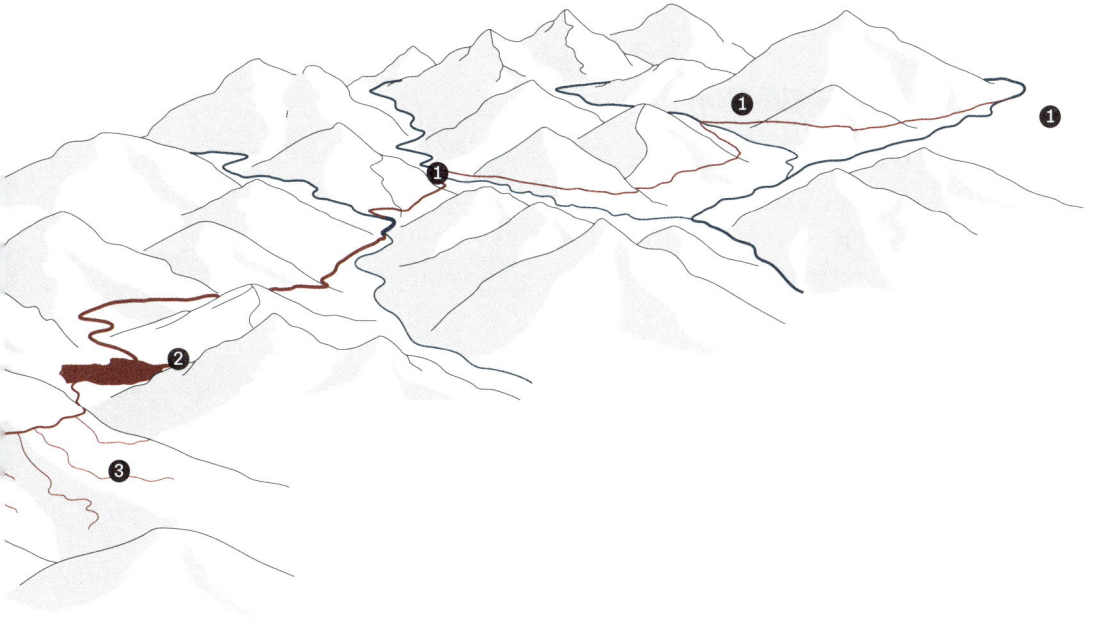

PARALLEL NARRATIVES FOR CITY AND BASIN

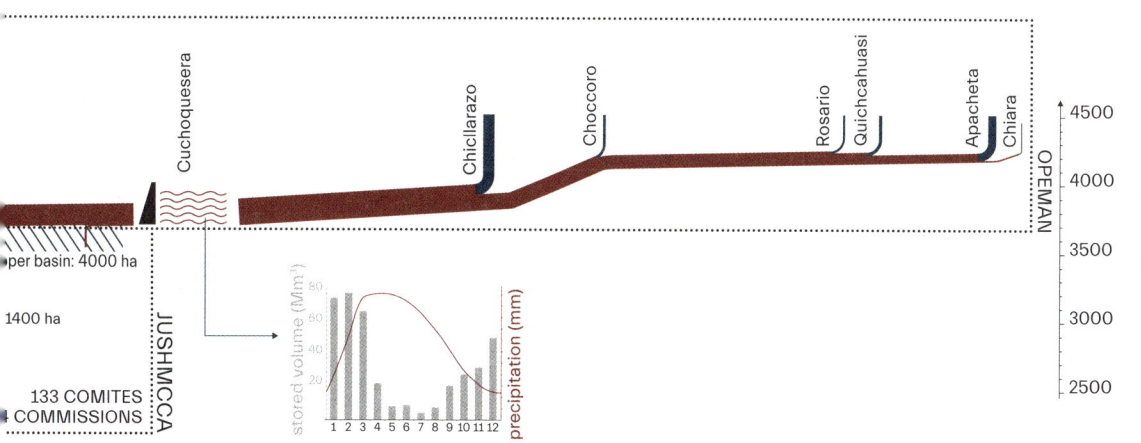

Data: Gobierno Regional de Ayacucho, 2006 & GESAAM, 2016

URBAN ANDES

2000 m
2500 m
3000 m
3500 m
4000 m
4500 m
3618.8 km²
21.7 km²
95.1 km²
74.6 km²
131.5 km²
HUANTA
86.1 km²
61.1 km²
13.4 km²
88.0 km²
67.3 km²
176.4 km²
WESTERN WATERSHED
28.6 km²
121.4 km²
AYACUCHO
16.0 km²
104.6 km²
8.9 km²
CENTRAL WATERSHED
CUENCA ALTA
SOCOS
CUENCA BAJA
55.5 km²
457.8 km²
176.4 km²
209.9 km²
PROYECTO RIO CACHI
42.7 km²
EASTERN WATERSHED
13.4 km²
28.9 km²
10.5 km²
25.7 km²
159.3 km²
240.0 km²
165.5 km²
260.0 km²
175.7 km²

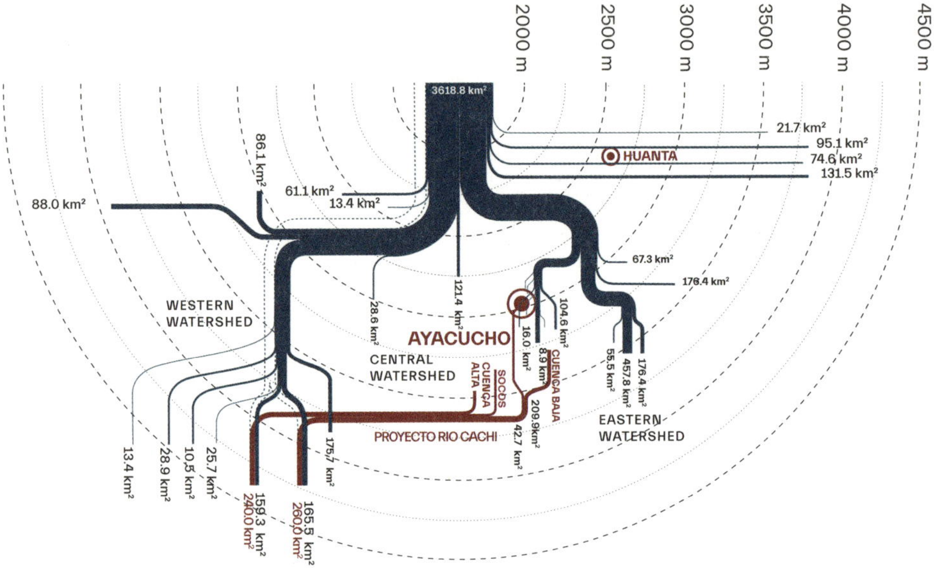

fig. 7

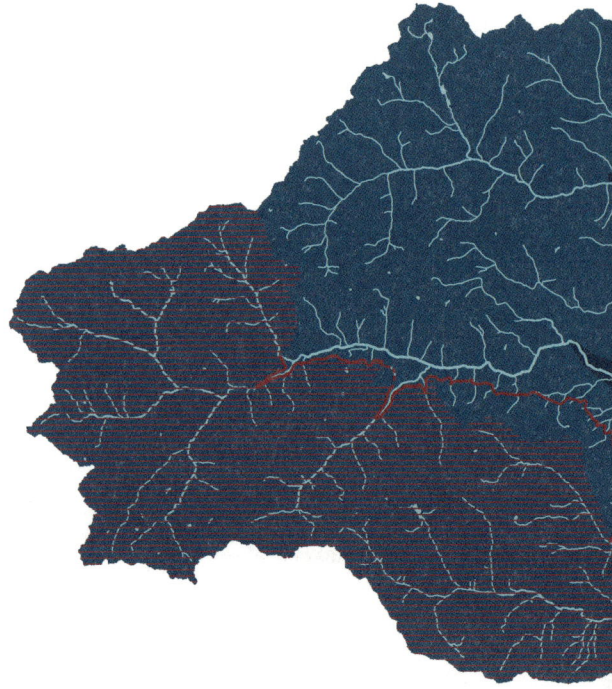

THE BASIN'S WATER STRUCTURE
CURRENT SITUATION:
river
lake
canal/tunnel
artificial reservoir
irrigation area
water extraction area
major rain area
dam
PLANNED INTERVENTIONS
canal
artificial reservoir
irrigation zone
water extraction area
Ayacucho's emergency water provision
1 AYACUCHO
2 HUANTA

fig. 8

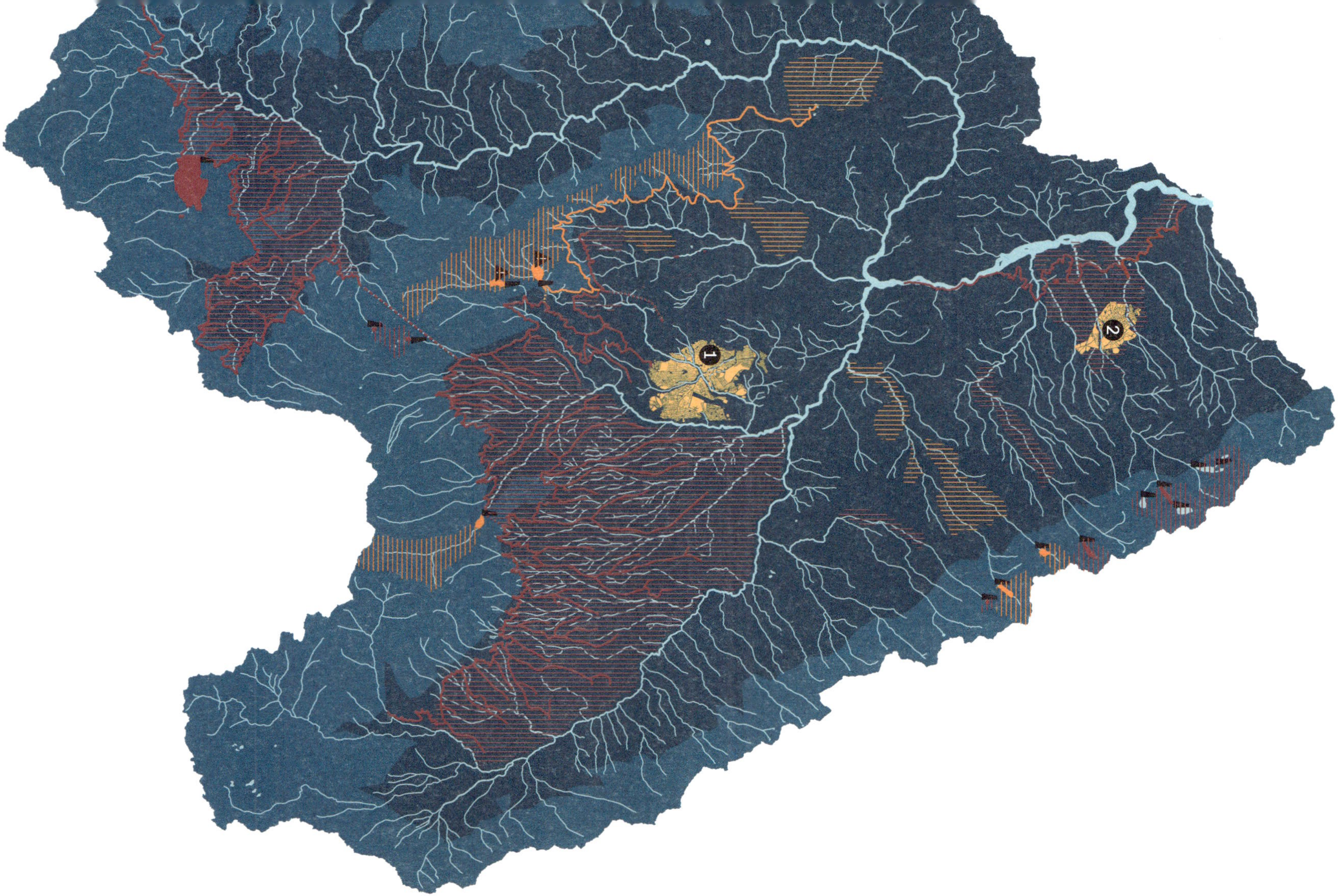

URBAN ANDES   PARALLEL NARRATIVES FOR CITY AND BASIN   33

Linear water management

The water harvested by means of the Cachi River Project[13] arrives in Ayacucho from the south, at the Quicapata reservoir and treatment plant.[14] From here, it is dispersed to reservoirs each supplying parts of the city with potable water. The size of these reservoirs has not always kept pace with the city's growth however. As a result, potable water supply in some neighbourhoods is rationed and only available for several hours a day, with frequent periods of water unavailability.

13 The Cachi River Project delivers up to 850 l/s of water to the city (*Gobierno Regional de Ayacucho*, 2006, p. 31).
14 As of 2019, a second treatment plant was under construction, to the west of the city.
15 SEDA, 2016
16 The plant's size was originally determined based on the 1980 census, with a design flow rate of 200 l/s. Current flow rate is estimated to average 500 l/s (interview with Meza Lazaro, SEDA, 2018).
17 Interview with Melisho Salas, manager for ALA (*Administración Local del Agua*) Ayacucho, 2018

Where the distribution network does not yet connect to individual plots, water is made available at communal taps. Some recent peripheral settlements are not connected to the potable water network at all, not in the least because they sometimes develop above the altitude of the existing reservoirs.

After use, the water distributed throughout the city is expelled as wastewater. In the best case, it travels via the sewage system to the wastewater treatment plant located in the valley below the city, from where it is discharged into the river. According to official figures from 2016, 80% of Ayacucho's inhabitants are connected to the sewage system.[15] Taking into account the city's numerous unregistered residents, the true number is even lower.

Furthermore, the flow rate of wastewater through the plant is far higher than its design capacity,[16] resulting in poor quality of the discharged water. As of 2019, an additional wastewater treatment plant is under construction to the north of the city, but its capacity is already insufficient for the current population.[17] The untreated and poorly treated wastewater expelled back into the hydrological system of the basin affects the communities, agriculture, and ecologies downstream.

Resisting the rain

Meanwhile, whereas much attention is given to harvesting rainwater from afar and bringing it to the city, precipitation falling during the short wet season within the urban area itself is treated with far less regard.

Ayacucho's outskirts read like a patchwork of gridded, unpaved roads, with one axis generally oriented parallel to the dominant slope of the terrain. The roads aligned in this way collect and restrain the surface runoff within their width. As a consequence, the rate of flow increases, cutting trenches into the roads and picking up soil and debris.

This is aggravated by the condition of the higher-lying open spaces. Here, due to overharvesting of vegetation–typically for construction or domestic use– the soil erodes, water retention capacity is diminished, and larger quantities of surface runoff are sent towards the city below.

The more built-up neighbourhoods feature paved roads. Although these improve mobility and accessibility, they also impede all infiltration and further increase the speed at which the surface runoff courses downwards. These large quantities of fast-flowing, debris-filled water cause local flooding and subsidence of buildings and roads. →fig. 9

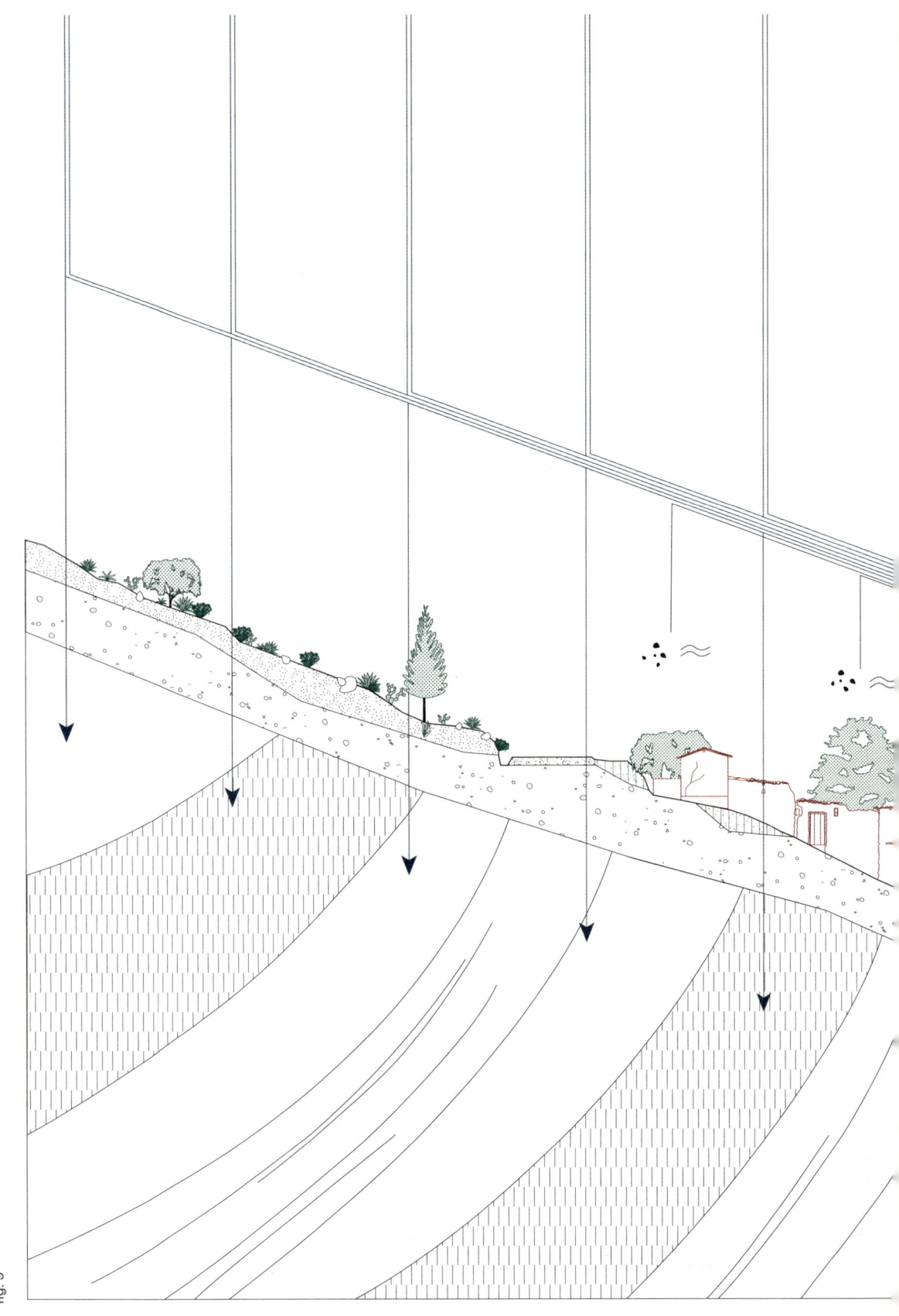
fig. 9

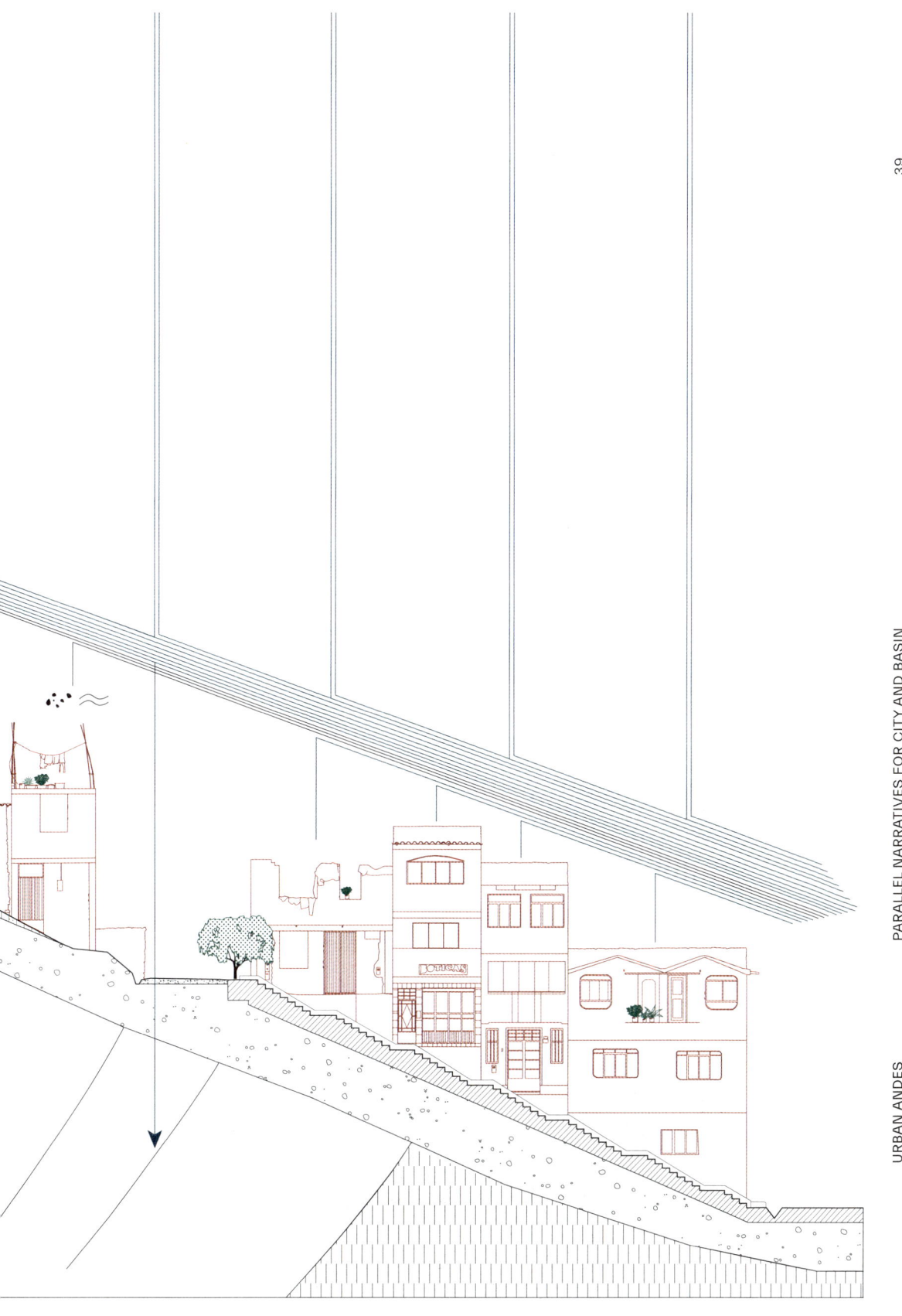

Following a calamitous mudslide and flood in 2009, a drainage system was installed in the city centre to collect and evacuate surface runoff. This system attempts to control the flow of water where it is strongest, risking severe consequences in the event of failure. It is also symptomatic of an approach aimed at moving water out of the city as fast as possible, effectively displacing the problem further downstream.

In many parts of the city centre, the rivers and dry creek beds[18] have been canalized and covered. In times of heavy rain, exacerbated by the continued deforestation and urbanization of the surrounding slopes, the reduced profile of the riverbed is unable to contain the amount of water flowing through it. Substantial areas in the city centre flood as a result.

This situation could be mitigated by allowing open areas in the city centre to participate in the retention of excess water in times of need. However, the majority of the public green spaces dotting the city are disconnected from larger hydrological networks. To the contrary, the lawns and exotic trees often planted in these green spaces have high water demands, and are most usually irrigated using potable water, putting further strain on the city's limited resources.

Legislation prohibiting construction in locations designated as vulnerable to flooding or landslides exists, but both awareness of the locations' boundaries and enforcement of the legislation itself is lacking. Construction continues, putting the urban fabric increasingly at odds with natural hydrology.

18 Dry creek beds are a typical phenomenon in the semi-arid sierra and go by many names depending on their specific characteristics and on local dialects: *arroyo, riochuelo, quebrada, torrentera*, etc.

Urban watershed

The superposition of topography and soil with the potable, waste- and rainwater networks creates an 'urban watershed': a hybrid natural/infrastructural hydrological system.
    It is clear that many components of this watershed are poorly coordinated, resulting in a contradictory situation wherein an almost constant shortage of water is punctuated by brief, intense moments of excess. It is equally clear that certain inhabitants of this watershed experience water privilege, to the detriment of others. The fortunate have unlimited access to potable water and are connected to the sewage system. The unfortunate either do not or are exposed to the risk of floods and landslides.
    With the urban watershed as a framework, new interventions can be planned which close water use circuits in order to bring supply and demand closer together; which rebalance the distribution of water-related risks and benefits; and which strategically position open space where it can play a role in buffering excess water. →fig. 10

URBAN ANDES • PARALLEL NARRATIVES FOR CITY AND BASIN

II.

ANDEAN MULTILOCALITY THROUGH TIME

Inhabiting multiple ecological zones

Peru is commonly divided into three broad climatic regions: *costa*, *sierra*, and *selva*. These terms are insufficiently precise, however, for understanding the regional settlement patterns that developed in the pre-Hispanic Andes, traces of which persist to this day.

The indigenous categorization of the territory into eight ecological zones offers the requisite precision.[19] From west to east, these are: *Chala* (or *Costa*), *Yunga*, *Quechua*, *Suni*, *Puna* (also called *Jalca*), and *Janca*. The eastern tropical forest contains the final two zones: *Rupa Rupa* and *Omagua*. This delimitation is largely defined by the ecological conditions at each altitude that allow for the cultivation of specific crops and the raising of different livestock. The altitudes listed in the scheme to the right can vary somewhat depending on local factors. →fig. 11

The harsh climatic conditions of the Andes made surviving in any single ecological zone nearly impossible. However, the mutual proximity of multiple ecological zones–a result of the extreme topography

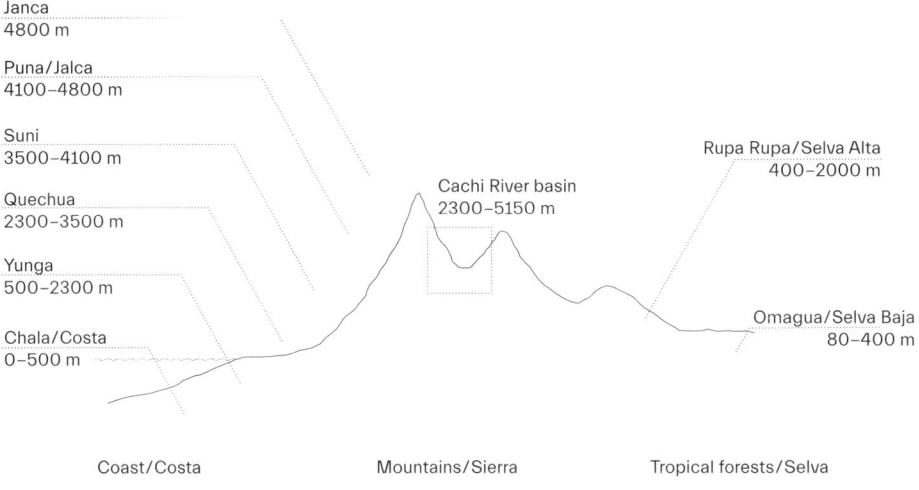

of the Andes– facilitated the emergence of multilocal communities. Each community strived for 'ecological complementarity': self-sufficiency through the direct control of a maximum number of ecological zones in order to acquire a sufficient diversity of natural resources.[20]

In order to manage these resources, communities would either migrate seasonally between settlements in different ecological zones, or would send households to permanently occupy outposts in zones away from the primary settlement. This pattern of dispersed multiple settlements with adjacent cultivated lands–'islands' within a larger, unoccupied territory– is known as the 'vertical archipelago'.[21]

Four of these ecological zones are present in the Cachi Basin: *Yunga, Quechua, Suni,* and *Puna*. The contemporary relevance of this division is evident when it is combined with current land cover maps[22]. The majority of agricultural activity still takes place in the *Quechua* zone, where modern staple crops such as potatoes, corn, beans, and wheat can be cultivated. This region is also where the basin's primary cities are located.

19   As identified by the ethnogeographer Javier Pulgar Vidal in *Las ocho regiones naturales del Perú* (first presented in 1941 and first published in 1946).

20   Murra, 1974, p. 94
21   Murra, 1974, p. 94
22   See the *Mapa Nacional de Cobertura Vegetal* issued by the Peruvian Ministry of Environment in 2015.

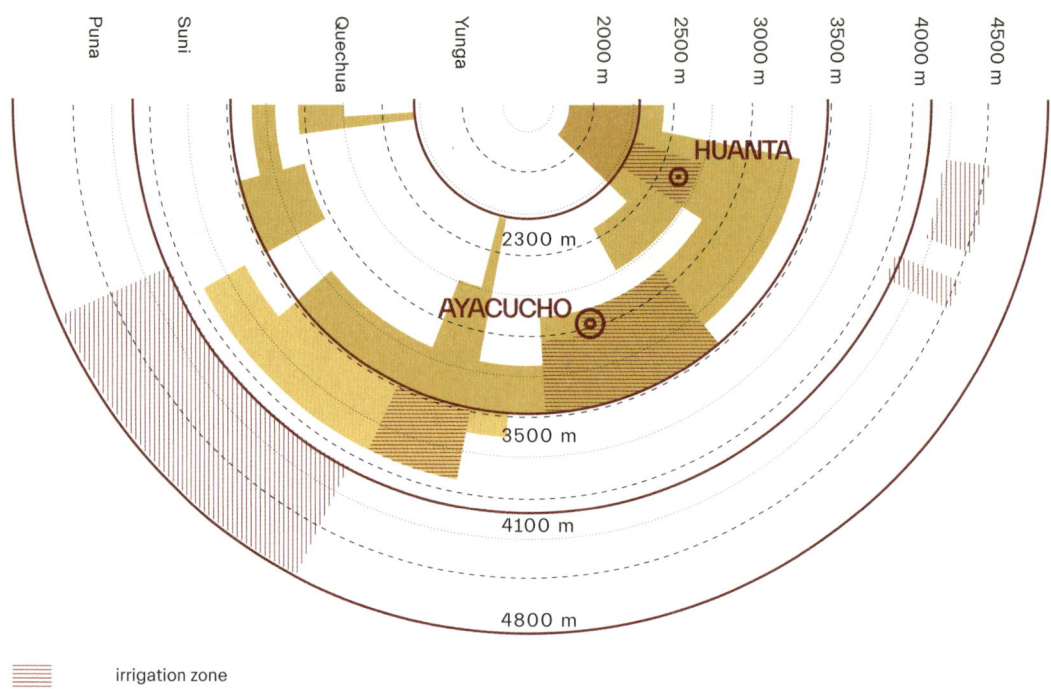

- irrigation zone
- extraction zone
- agriculture in Yunga
- agriculture in Quechua
- agriculture in Suni

PUNA (4100–4800 M)
cattle

SUNI (3500–4100 M)
quinua, potatoes, olluco

QUECHUA (2300–3500 M)
corn, cabbage, beans, wheat

YUNGA (2300–3500 M)
fruit, avocados, tomatoes, carrots

fig. 12

BASIN ECOLOGIES
- glaciers
- no vegetation
- wetland
- grassland
- bushes
- forest
- agriculture
- irrigation zone
- extraction zone

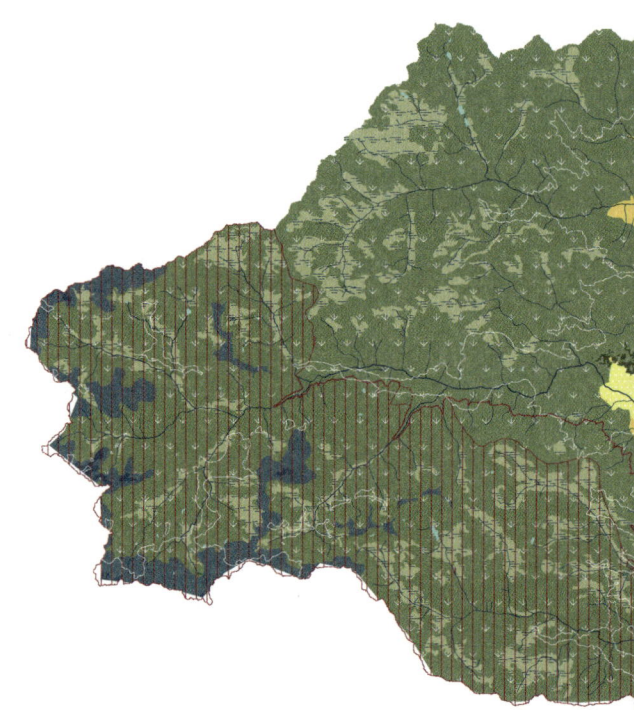

fig. 13

No fields are found in the *Puna* zone, nor are there forests: this is grassland, primarily used for livestock herding. →fig. 12-13

Societies of exchange and exploitation

Key within the societal structure of the vertical archipelago was that each household of the community retained the right to a share of produce from all ecological zones,

23 Referred to as 'redistribution' by Murra (Murra, 2017).
24 Which Murra refers to as 'reciprocity' (Murra, 2017).
25 Murra, 2017, p. 74
26 Murra, 2017, p. 75
27 See the act of *yarqa aspiy* as described by Chagnollaud (Chagnollaud, 2016, p. 217).
28 Zapata Velasco et al., 2008
29 Chagnollaud, 2016, p. 33
30 Chagnollaud, 2016, p. 33

not just from the zone(s) that they themselves cultivated.²³ There was virtually no trade of goods within communities. Rather, labour time was exchanged.²⁴

The complexity and diversity of these exchanges is reflected in the many names associated with them: *ayni, mink'a, mit'a, yanapa. Ayni* refers to a private exchange of equivalent labour between two households.²⁵ *Mit'a* is labour owed to the community or to the larger state by each household,²⁶ for example, for the construction of common infrastructure like roads or irrigation channels.

Variants of these reciprocal practices still exist in some rural communities, although communal labour is now typically called *faena*, meaning 'task' or 'chore' in Spanish. A typical example is the annual cleaning of irrigation channels, an event which is combined with rituals and festivities.²⁷

The spatial and societal structure of Andean communities was challenged by the arrival of the Spaniards and the imposition of a colonial model of territorial management and control. Huamanga–the future city of Ayacucho–was founded in 1540 at the halfway point between Lima and Cuzco. From here, the Spanish could exert power over the region and oversee agricultural and mining activities.²⁸ The colonizers also sought to forcefully relocate the dispersed indigenous population toward neighbourhoods at the city's edge, so as to facilitate their control, conversion, and taxation,²⁹ and to claim ownership of abandoned land higher up in the headlands.

The foundation of Huamanga marked the start of a transition from a multilocal, rural settlement pattern to a more centralized urban system, which is still ongoing, as demonstrated by the city's continued growth today. The dominant system of exchange shifted from the exchange of labour to that of goods. Certain principles of reciprocity were manipulated for the colonizers' gain. For example, *mit'a* became *mita minera*, a form of forced labour in mines.³⁰ Equivalent exchange became asymmetrical exploitation of labour.

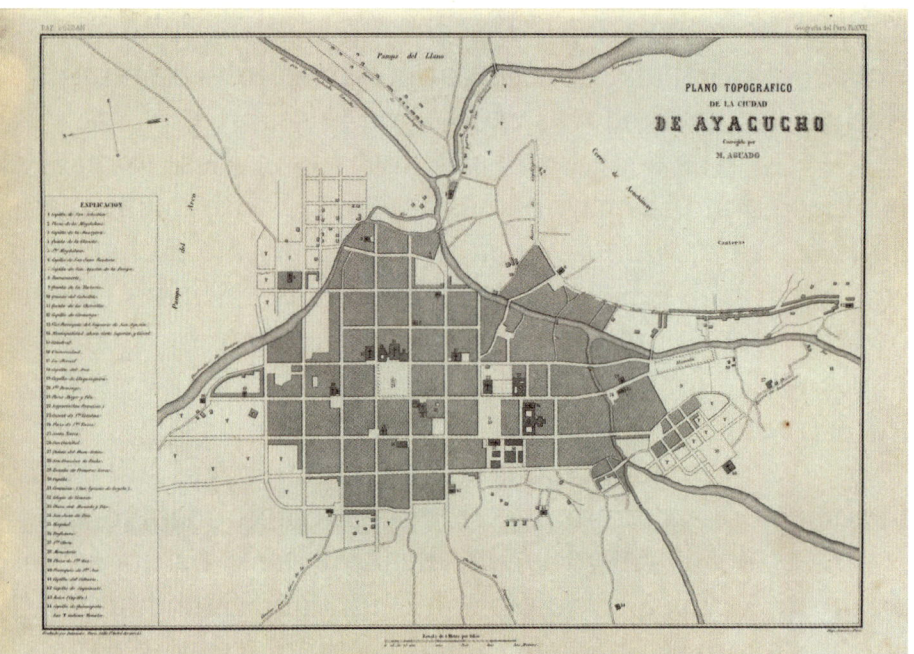

Twentieth-century rural/urban migration

Although its fortunes fluctuated over the course of the following centuries, in 1940 the city by then known as Ayacucho was an isolated regional centre of roughly 18.000 inhabitants, its limits hardly different from those of the original sixteenth-century colonial settlement.[31]

Three important factors would soon change this status, however: the improving interregional road network; →fig. 14-15 the availability of secondary and higher education in the city;[32] and the success in the 1960s of popular movements advocating for granting ownership rights to tenants of municipal terrain in the urban periphery. By 1981, rural migration had caused the urban population to rise to 69.533.[33]

---

31 Chagnollaud, 2016, p. 32
32 With the reopening of the Universidad Nacional de San Cristóbal de Huamanga (UNSCH) in 1959 as key event.
33 Bejar Romero, Pereyra Chavez, 2006, p. 172
34 In Spanish, *El Sendero Luminoso*, a far-left guerrilla movement.
35 Bejar Romero, Pereyra Chavez, 2006, p. 172
36 Chagnollaud, 2010, p. 199

The armed conflict between the Shining Path[34] and the Peruvian state, which started in the region surrounding Ayacucho in 1981, prompted a further increase in migration towards the relative safety of the city. By 1993–at which time the epicentre of the conflict was shifting towards Lima–Ayacucho's urban population had risen to 114.809[35].

Many of the people who settled in Ayacucho's periphery in the '80s and '90s chose to remain even after the resolution of the armed conflict. However, in many cases they have retained strong links to their ancestral villages and to rural life.[36] Some still work in the fields outside of the city. The proliferation of motorized transport means a daily commute between urban periphery and rural place

.... 3 hour action radius in 1950
- - - - 3 hour action radius in 1990
- - - 3 hour action radius in 2018

fig. 14

OWNERSHIP STRUCTURE
- community-owned land
- private- or government-owned land

COMMUTING DISTANCE
- 45 minutes car drive radius
- 1,5 hour car drive radius
- primary roads
- secondary roads
- rivers

POPULATION
- less than 10 inhabitants
- 10–40 inhabitants
- 40–70 inhabitants
- 70–500 inhabitants
- 500–2000 inhabitants
- 40 000 inhabitants (Huanta)

150 000 inhabitants (Ayacucho)

fig. 15

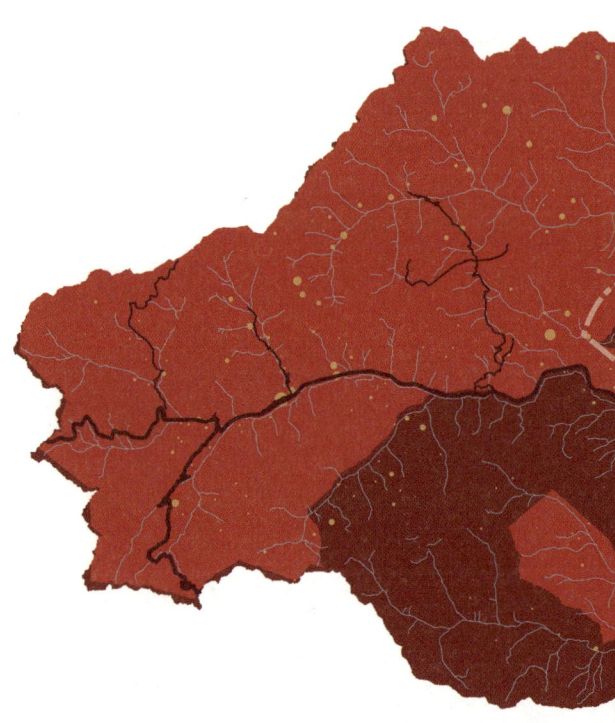

of work is possible, although some labourers migrate between city and countryside according to the rhythm of the harvests.

Inversely, inhabitants of the surrounding villages sometimes take jobs in Ayacucho–for example, in construction–or go back and forth to sell agricultural produce or other goods, as well as to buy products that are only available in the city. Education remains an important urban attractor for younger rural dwellers. Depending on travel time and on the extent of their urban network, these people may likewise opt for either daily commutes or for more extended stays in the city.[37]

Modern multilocality?

There are interesting parallels between this modern multilocality and the historic network of the vertical archipelago, with Ayacucho playing either the role of central settlement or that of multi-ethnic outpost, depending on the point of view of the actors involved.

However, there are also important differences. The principle of redistribution–the idea that each member of the community has a right to a share of all of the community's produce–is virtually absent. Equally absent is the ambition to achieve ecological complementarity. To the contrary, projects such as the previously discussed Cachi River Project are a clear attempt to prioritize the area around Ayacucho, at the expense of other, more distant ecological zones.

Nevertheless, it is crucial to recognize that the periphery is not mono-oriented towards the centre, but that it forms a social and economic interface between the city and the surrounding territory of the Cachi Basin. Interventions must be conceived looking both inwards and outwards.

Methods of urban expansion: piecemeal purchasing

Ayacucho's strong demographic growth has gone hand in hand with a primarily horizontal urban expansion, the dominant methods of which have evolved over time. In the 1950s and '60s, the main methods were the piecemeal purchase and development of land from private owners (mainly the *haciendas*[38] surrounding the city), and the parcellation and renting of municipal terrain.[39]

In the case of the neighbourhood of EMADI, established in the 1960s, local government even took on an active role in its planning and development.[40] The neighbourhood was designed according to the modernist 'superblock' model: a dense cluster of housing blocks veined by a network of pedestrian alleys and small parks and plazas. However, this type of publicly initiated urban development would not be repeated. →fig. 16

---

37 Chagnollaud, 2010, p. 200
38 Large, colonial-era farms.
39 Chagnollaud, 2016, pp. 51; 54
40 Interview with Quintas Mendez, 2018

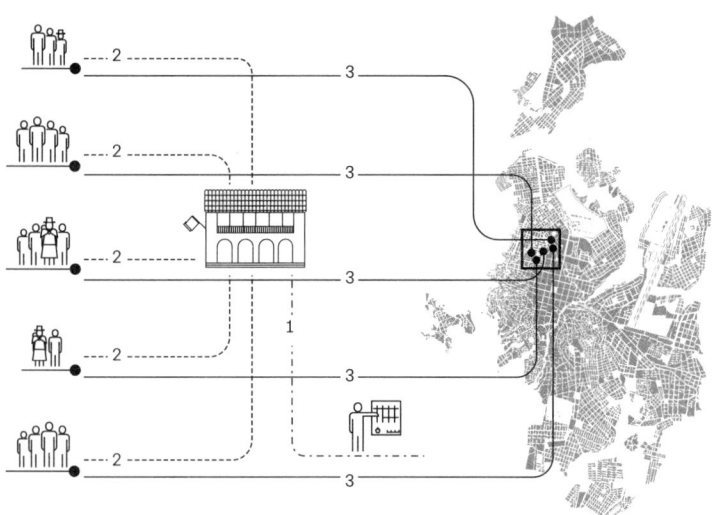

fig. 16

DEVELOPMENT OF EMADI
NEIGHBOURHOOD

Phase 1   The municipality organizes the layout and landownership of the site.
Phase 2   The future dwellers negotiate with the municipality to buy a plot.
Phase 3   People start to build on their new property.

Methods of urban expansion:
land invasions

In contrast to other Peruvian cities, primarily Lima, the founding of popular settlements[41] via extralegal land invasions of municipal or private terrain only started playing a significant role in Ayacucho following the expropriation of the surrounding *haciendas* effectuated by the Agrarian Reform Act of 1969.[42]

Land invasions would become the primary method of settlement for the rural refugees fleeing armed conflict in the '80s and '90s. During this period, resistance to land invasions was limited due to an absence of state control and the departure of many private landowners.[43]

The majority of popular settlements was regularized by the national government in 1999 and 2000, in an attempt to return to a situation of conventional legality. This policy arguably led to the perceived validation of land invasions as a settlement model, however, and they continue to be the principal driver of urban expansion in Ayacucho today.[44]

Contemporary land invasions in Ayacucho are coordinated affairs. They are planned well in advance by organized groups, consisting mainly of younger urban inhabitants wishing to found their own household.[45]

Several hundred people are typically involved in the actual invasion, and once the terrain is successfully occupied a pre-established scheme is laid out that includes a private parcel (often measuring ca. 10×20 meters) for each *socio*[46] and space for collective amenities such as a church, school, or football pitch. Construction of the occupants' housing starts immediately. The goal is to 'consolidate' the terrain and be recognized by the municipality as an *Asentamiento Humano*.[47] This statute allows the new community to negotiate access to utilities and to start the administrative process requesting legal ownership of the terrain.[48]

A representative example of such a case is the neighbourhood of Mollepata I, founded on a hill to the north of the city centre in 2002. →fig. 17-18 Originally an invasion of privately owned land, negotiations between the legal owner, the occupants, and the state were still ongoing in 2018.[49]

41 This term is a translation of the Spanish *urbanizaciones populares*, which is often used in this context, including in Peruvian law. It is an alternative to 'informal settlements', a term which seems to marginalize what is in fact the main form of urban development in many Andean cities, including Ayacucho.
42 Chagnollaud, 2016, p. 58
43 Chagnollaud, 2016, pp.66-67; 79
44 Chagnollaud, 2016, p. 73
45 Chagnollaud, 2016, p. 77
46 A member of the land invasion group, generally a representative of a single household.
47 Spanish for 'human settlement'.
48 For a detailed description of the organizational structure and different steps of a land invasion, see Chagnollaud, 2016, pp. 83-98.
49 Interview with German, 2018

DEVELOPMENT OF MOLLEPATA I

Phase 1   Different families group together to organize a land invasion.
Phase 2   They define the future layout and define the plots.
Phase 3   There is no negotiation with the landowner in advance.
Phase 4   The families claim their land in a coordinated invasion.

TISSUE SAMPLE

❶ standard plot: 10×20 m
❷ central market
❸ domestic wastewater collected in gullies in the street

fig. 17

fig. 18

In order to consolidate the occupied terrain as quickly as possible, its new residents must work together to fabricate the adobe bricks necessary to start construction of their houses. This exchange of labour between households is structured according to the principles of *ayni*,[50] mobilizing this pre-colonial, rural practice as an essential step in the foundation of new communities in a modern-day urban context.

Methods of urban expansion: allotments

In other instances, private landowners choose to develop their own allotment plans and sell plots to individual buyers. The neighbourhood of Mollepata II is such an

50 Chagnollaud, 2016, pp. 93; 169

DEVELOPMENT OF MOLLEPATA II

Phase 1 The landowner commissions a plan for the site.
Phase 2 The future dwellers negotiate with landowner to buy a plot.
Phase 3 People are entitled and start to build on their new property.

TISSUE SAMPLE

1. original plot (°2005)
2. plot in new plan (°2011)
3. original pathways
4. new road network

example. →fig. 19–20 Because ownership of the plots is official, there is no need to consolidate the terrain. Plots are sometimes acquired as a financial investment, and can remain unoccupied for multiple years.[51] This situation helps to explain why Mollepata II is markedly less built-up and has less access to utilities than Mollepata I, even though its development started in 2005, only three years after the foundation of Mollepata I.

A final type of urban expansion is represented by the neighbourhood of Yanama and combines aspects of the previous two methods. In the early 2000s, a citizen collective legally purchased a large parcel of land to the south of the city. They drafted their own development plan and divided the plots among themselves. →fig. 21

This has resulted in a very regular plan layout with perfectly rectangular plots, some of which remain empty: similar to Mollepata II, the undisputed ownership of each plot means there is no urgency to commence construction.

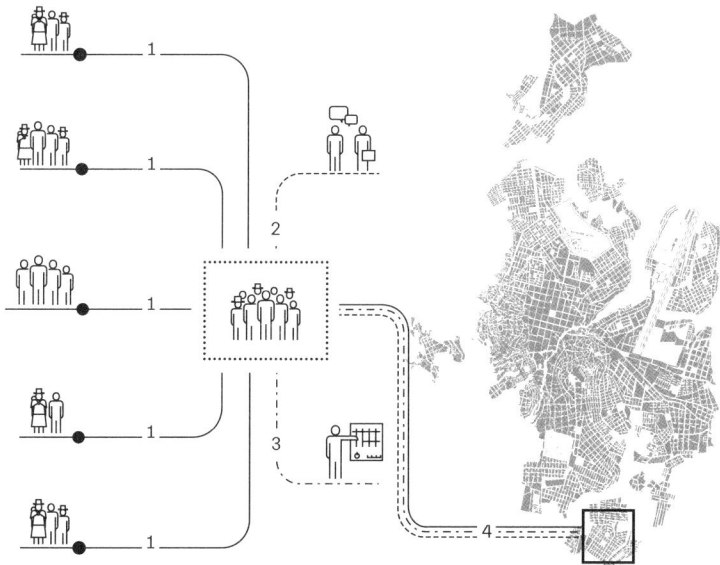

DEVELOPMENT OF YANAMA

Phase 1 Different families form a collective.
Phase 2 The collective negotiates with the landowner.
Phase 3 The collective drafts a plan.
Phase 4 The families purchase a plot and construct their house.

51 Interview with Flors Bejerano, 2018

Urban *faena*

Very often, the newly founded neighbourhoods lack basic utilities: electricity, potable water, sewage. This is either due to a scarcity of municipal funds or due to the community not yet being officially recognized. In the end, these services are often obtained through a routine deal: the utilities company provides the necessary materials, and the community provides the labour force.[52]

Remarkably, *Asentamientos Humanos* often seem to obtain access to utilities faster than regular neighbourhoods do. Indeed, the strong social structures necessary to plan and sustain a successful land invasion allow for continued community-level organization. Similar to the invocation of *ayni* in the first weeks of a land invasion, this process represents the urban reappropriation of another Andean concept of reciprocity: that of *faena*, or communal labour.[53]

This observation underscores the importance of this culture of reciprocity as a resource, especially in situations where official institutions are unable to regulate development or provide expected services. It must play a central role in a renewed vision of the sustainable growth of Ayacucho.

[52] Chagnollaud, 2016, p. 94   [53] Chagnollaud, 2016, p. 94

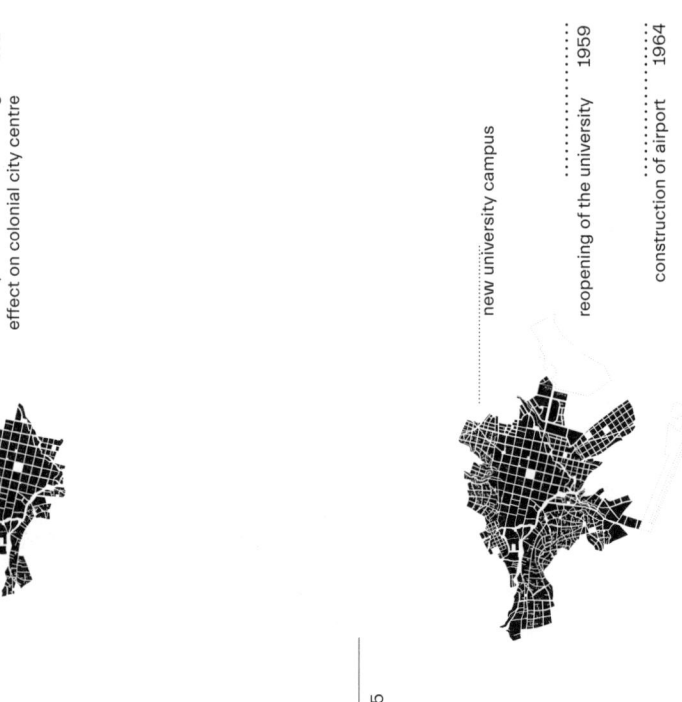

earthquake with devastating effect on colonial city centre   1914

new university campus
reopening of the university   1959
construction of airport   1964

1900–1940

1940–1975

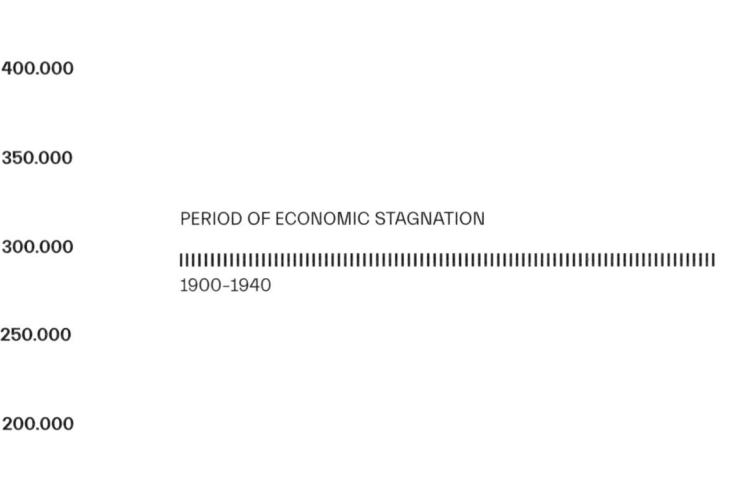

400.000

350.000

PERIOD OF ECONOMIC STAGNATION
|||||||||||||||||||||||||||||||||||||||||||||||||||||||||||||||||||||||
1900–1940

300.000

250.000

200.000

150.000

100.000

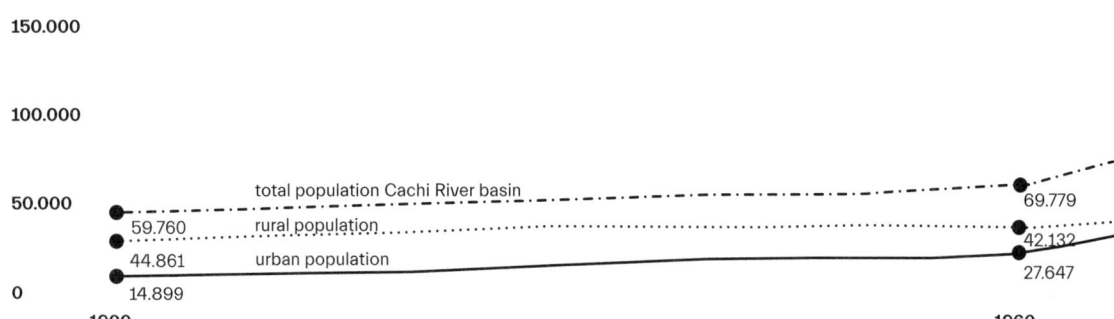

50.000 — total population Cachi River basin — 69.779
59.760 — rural population — 42.132
44.861 — urban population
0 — 14.899 — 27.647
1900   1960

fig. 22

Agrarian Reform Act 1969
series of earthquakes 1980
start construction Cachi River Project 1984

1975-2000

2000-2019

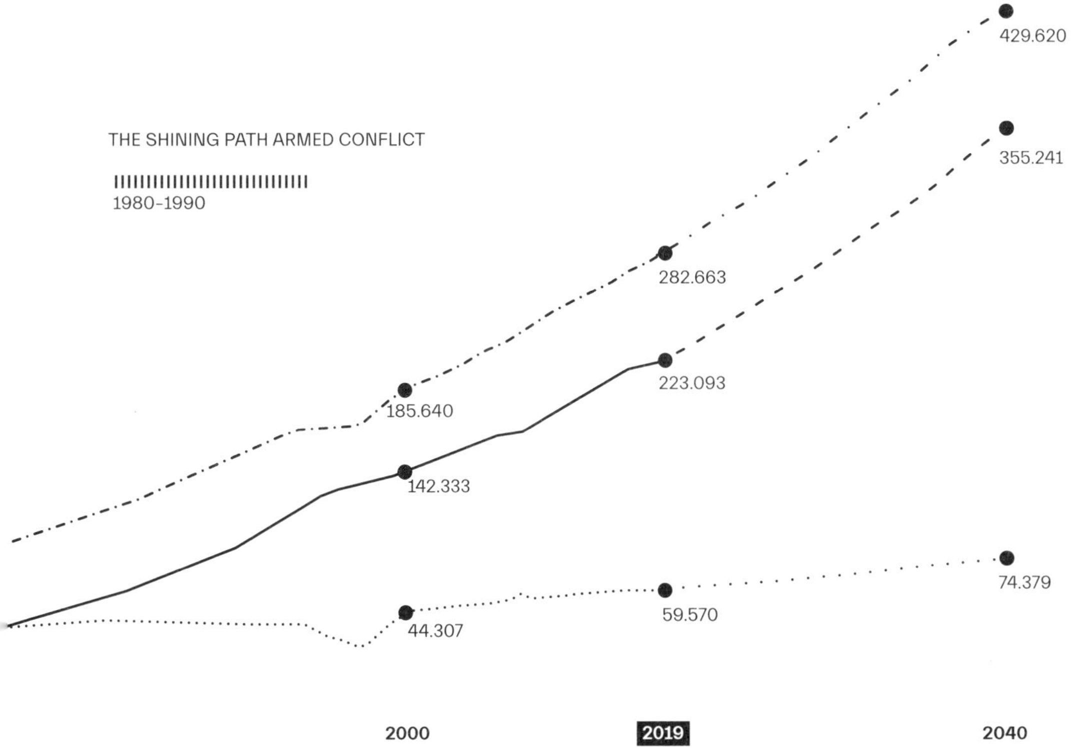

THE SHINING PATH ARMED CONFLICT
|||||||||||||||||||||||||||||||
1980-1990

429.620
355.241
282.663
223.093
185.640
142.333
74.379
59.570
44.307

2000   2019   2040

Data: SEDA, 2014 & INEI, 2016

PARALLEL NARRATIVES FOR CITY AND BASIN

URBAN ANDES

65

III.

PREPARING THE GROUND

Challenges to settling in the Andes have always been related to water and topography. Irrigation and terracing have played key roles in every Andean civilization since at least the Wari,[54] and they are still crucial today.

Irrigation

No permanent settlements can exist without cultivation of crops, and in the Andes this means providing agricultural fields with sufficiently fertile soil and a regular supply of water despite the large seasonal fluctuations in precipitation. Natural, vernacular, and large-scale systems of water retention have already been discussed in a previous chapter, and this water must still find its way to the crops themselves.

Today, of the 218.000 ha of agricultural land in the region of Ayacucho, 84.000 ha (39%) is irrigated.[55] The vast majority of this land uses a centuries-old technique of small channels and manually operated sluices. Crops are planted on slightly raised beds, and the interlaying ditches are regularly flooded. →fig. 23-24 An estimated 1,0 l/s/ha of water is required for this system to function, depending on crop type.[56]

More modern techniques such as sprinklers or drip irrigation could cut this to 0,5-0,7 l/s/ha[57]: a significant reduction in an increasingly water-stressed environment. However, only 1.700 ha[58]–less than 1% of total agricultural land–uses either of these systems. The principal cause for this paucity is that both techniques

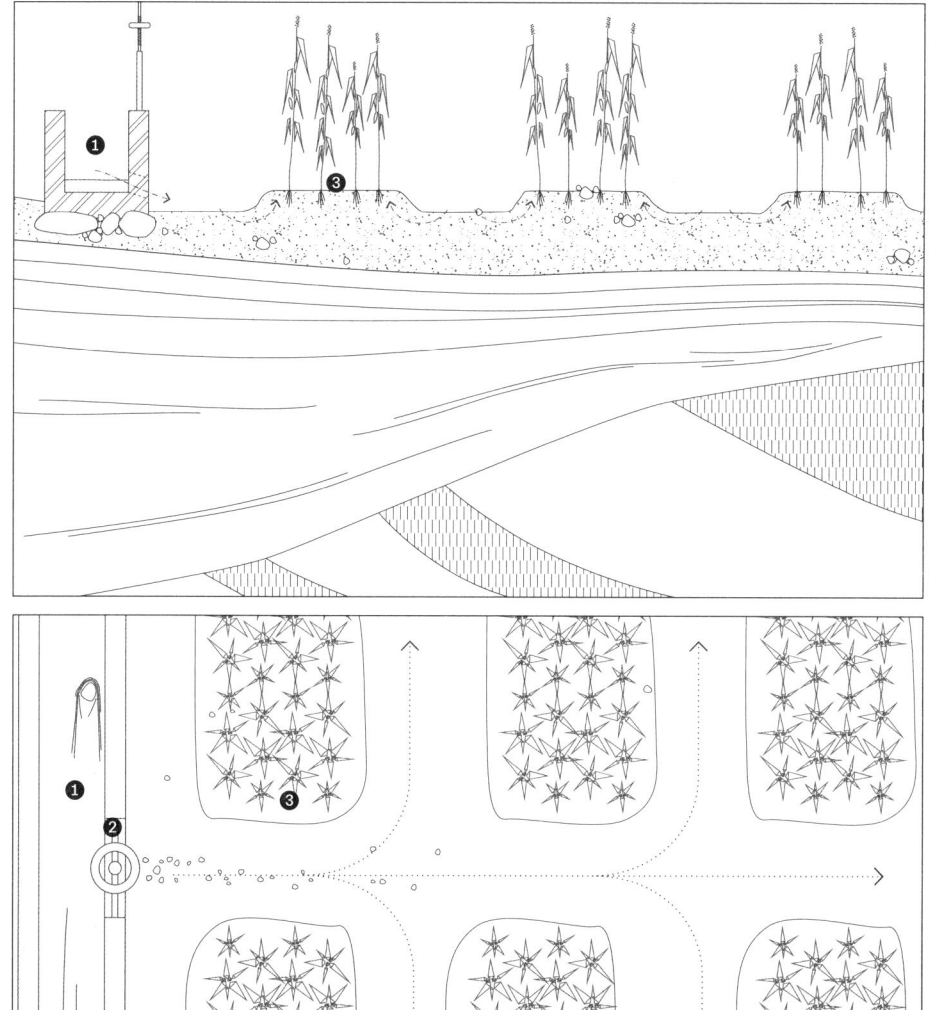

① concrete canal
② sluice
③ raised plant bed

54 The Wari controlled a large portion of modern-day Peru from ca. 500 to 1000 AD. The site of their capital city is located 11 km to the north-east of Ayacucho.

55 Interview with Barturen Ocampo, manager for PSI (*Programa Subsectorial de Irrigaciones*), 2018

56 Interview with Barturen Ocampo, PSI, 2018

57 Interview with Barturen Ocampo, PSI, 2018

58 Interview with Barturen Ocampo, PSI, 2018

require a much larger initial investment to install local water reservoirs, flux control systems, and the sprinklers or drip tubes themselves. The various components of both systems also require regular maintenance, and finding replacement parts can be a challenge in remote areas of the Andes.

Terracing

Still, the water necessary for crop growth also poses a risk: the thin layer of topsoil, located on the steep slopes of the Andes, is highly susceptible to erosion. Terracing is an essential technique to retain this topsoil and guarantee the continued fertility of Andean agricultural land.

Various types of anti-erosion strategies have been developed since pre-colonial times,[59] and the continued cultivation of some ancient terraces testifies to their durability. The most simple technique is the *zanja*: a shallow ditch (ca. 30 cm deep and 40 cm wide) dug perpendicular to the slope every five to ten meters. →fig. 25-26 These ditches slow water coursing downwards and retain sediments.

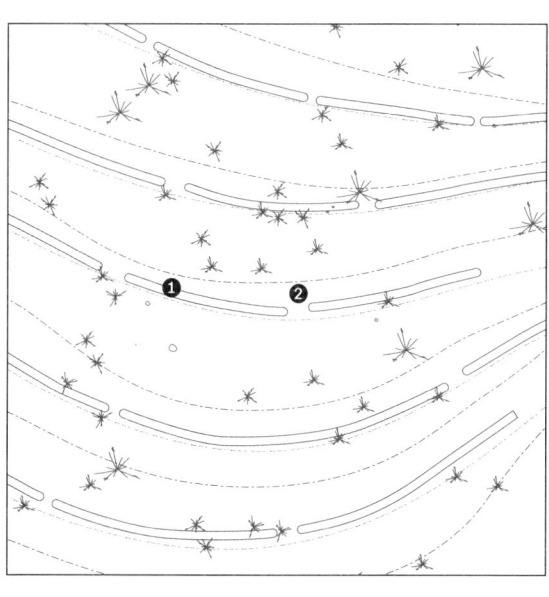

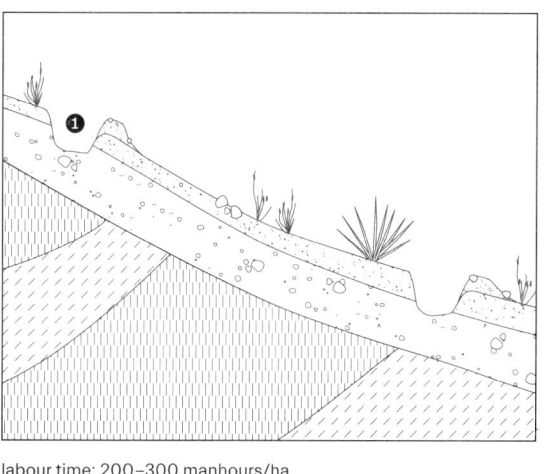

labour time: 200–300 manhours/ha

❶ *zanja* or shallow ditch
❷ interruption in *zanja* to avoid a lateral water flow

[59] The technical reference used for elaboration of all schemes related to terracing and erosion control is a manual written by J. Alanya Arango in 1998, on behalf of the Ministry of Agriculture: *Manual para Conservación de Suelos en Microcuencas Alto Andinas*. All estimated labour times mentioned in the following figures also derive from this source.

The *zanjas* are divided into segments with a length of approximately ten meters to avoid lateral water flow and must be cleared of sediments yearly.

A second technique is that of the 'slow-forming' terraces. As the name implies, these structures form over time. A first wall with a height of 70 to 100 cm is created perpendicular to the slope of the terrain, using available earth or stones. →fig. 27-28 The walls form erosion barriers, trapping sediment travelling downhill. As the sediment accumulates, the wall must be successively heightened. Given enough time, the slow-forming terraces create themselves. As a result, this technique is relatively labour-efficient.

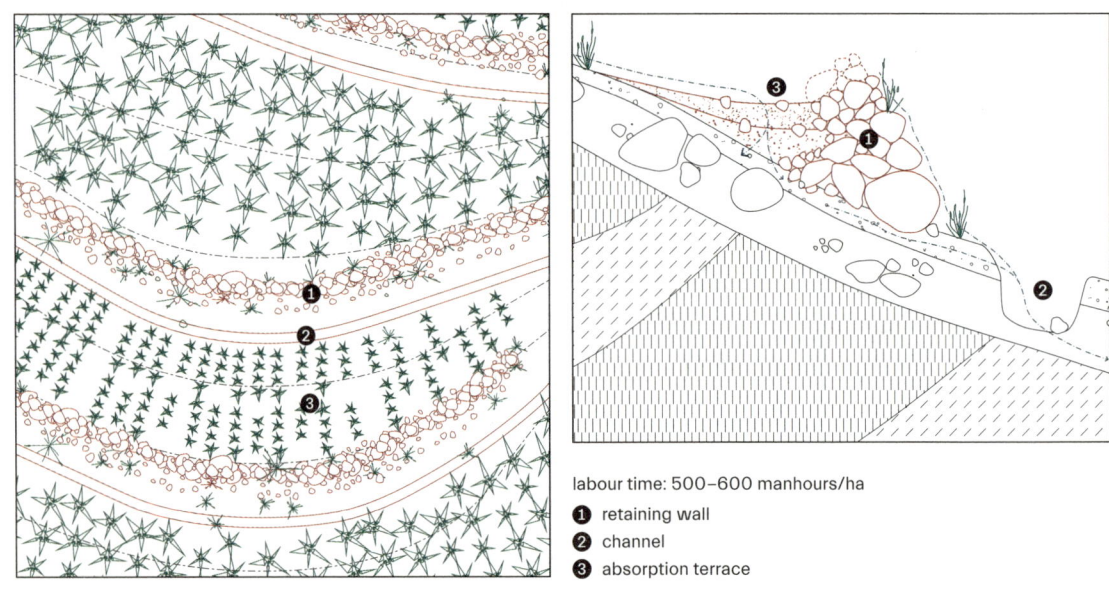

labour time: 500–600 manhours/ha
❶ retaining wall
❷ channel
❸ absorption terrace

Terraces can also be constructed all at once. Their man-high retaining walls are built of earth or stones. Earthen walls can be reinforced by adding plants, whose roots will hold the soil together. Important when applying this technique is to keep the different soil layers separated during construction. The original topsoil must be reused as the finishing layer of the horizontal terraces, as it is the most fertile. →fig. 29-30 The relatively large quantity of excavated soil means this technique requires a high amount of labour.

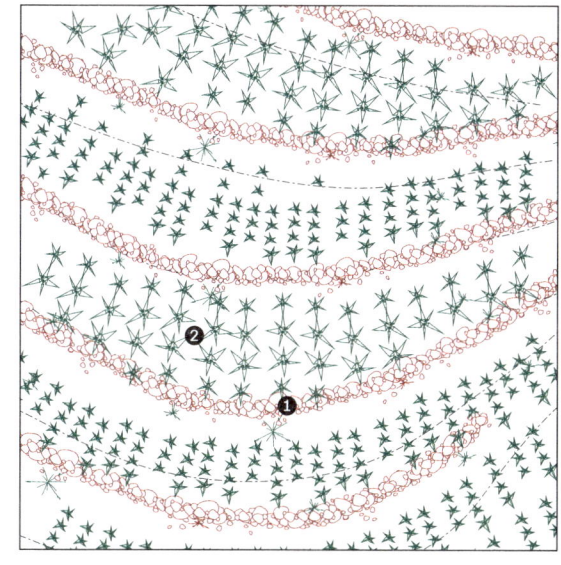 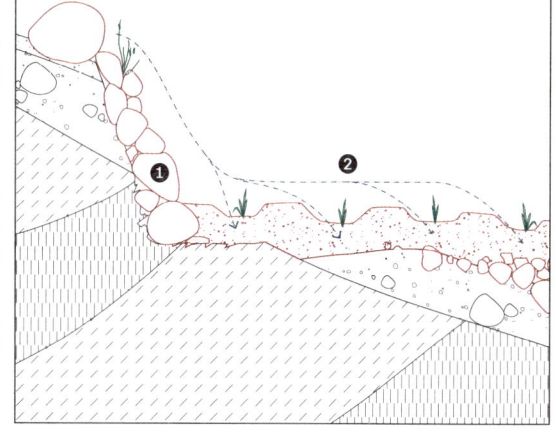

labour time: 1200–1500 manhours/ha
❶ retaining wall
❷ absorption terrace

On slopes where vegetation or anti-erosion measures are absent, erosion will quickly create gullies. During rainfall, water collects here and flows downward at high speeds, displacing large amounts of sediment and threatening foundations of adjacent construction as well as any form of settlement below it.

This formation of gullies can be mitigated using two techniques, both based on reducing flow rates and retaining sediment. One is to construct a series of small walls over the width of the gully. These walls function in the same way as the slow-forming terraces. A second approach is to plant trees and shrubs in the gully. Their roots retain the soil, while their trunks and branches slow the flow of water. →fig. 31-34 In both cases it is important to take the force of the water into account. Once the water has amassed too much strength, it is likely to tear down any obstacle, potentially creating an even more dangerous situation further downstream.

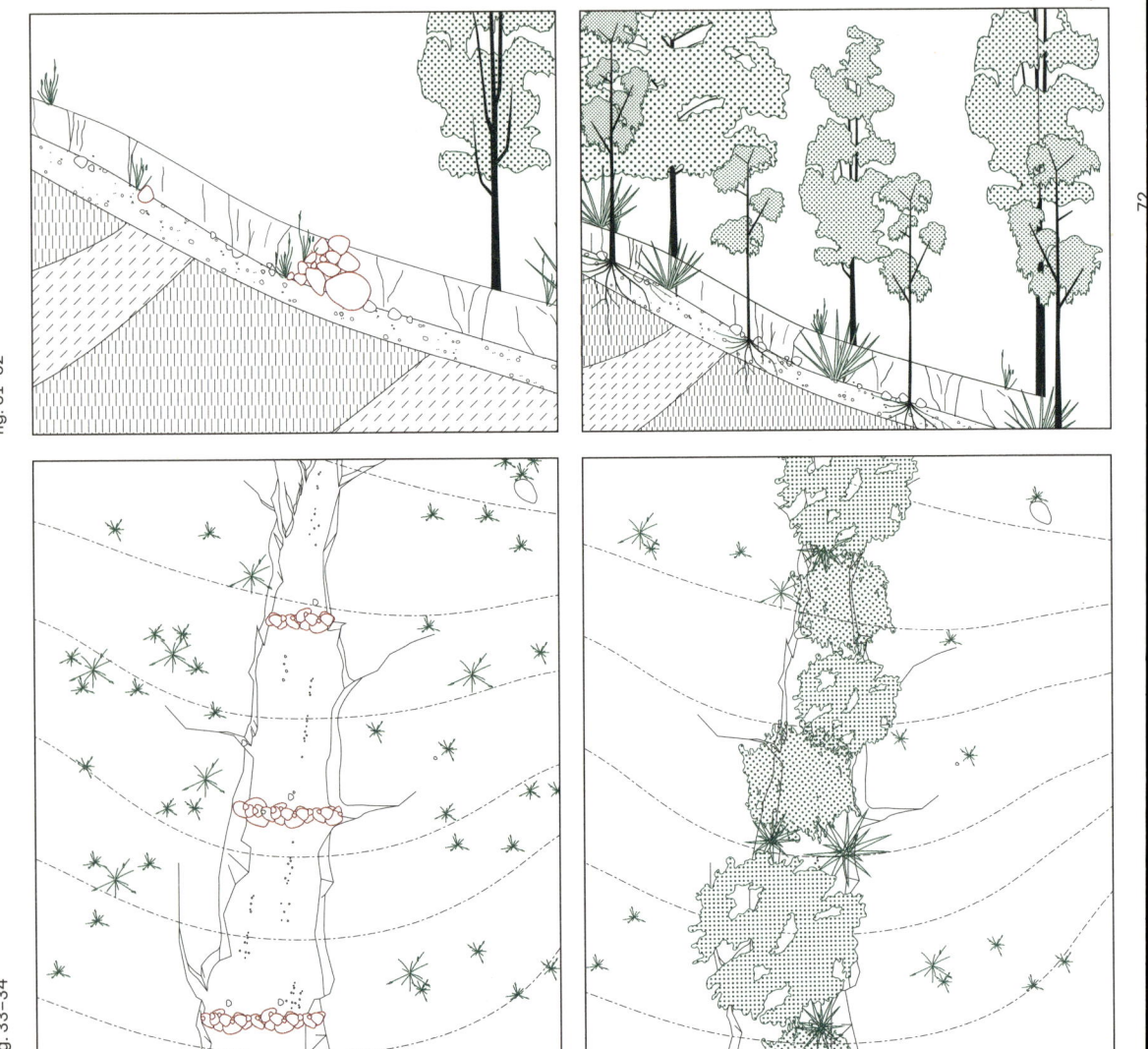

Talking maps and tactical trees

Recently, in the Cachi Basin and elsewhere, rural communities have started to rehabilitate the aforementioned traditional techniques. They are supported by governmental organizations and NGOs,[60] part of a broader ambition to develop agricultural practices that are both ecologically and economically sustainable.

Discussions often take place around so-called *mapas parlantes*–literally 'talking maps'–elaborated by the community members themselves. These collaborative, highly accessible maps are used to plan crop rotation and production strategies, develop business plans to receive funding, and ensure knowledge transfer. Their use is well-established, and they play an important role in building awareness and a sense of agency with regard to complex water and agricultural challenges. Such cartography has become an explicit method to enable communities, as well as to conserve and activate the tacit knowledge embedded in land cultivation and landscape maintenance.

One strategy that is receiving particular attention is the planting of trees and shrubs. The goal here is generally two-fold. On the one hand, many of these plants yield fruits, lumber, firewood, and raw materials for household or medicinal products. On the other hand, they mitigate erosion and surface runoff, function as windbreaks, and help to create a beneficial microclimate for crops or livestock.

60 Amongst them CEDAP (*Centro de Desarrollo Agropecuario*), INIA (*Instituto Nacional de Innovación Agraria*) and Agro Rural.

It must be mentioned that this strategy is not without risk. Some Andean afforestation initiatives employ fast-growing, exotic species–mainly pine (*Pinus patula* and *Pinus radiata*) and eucalyptus (*Eucalyptus globulus*). A recent study[61] has shown that although this reduces peak flows following rainfall (one of the primary drivers of gully formation), it also significantly reduces the total (subsurface) runoff within the afforested catchment areas, especially during the dry season.[62] In other words, these species extract a high amount of water from the soil, depriving downstream ecosystems and settlements of its potential use.

61 Ochoa-Tocachi et al., 2016
62 The aforementioned study found that low flows were reduced seven–to tenfold in comparison to a 'pristine' catchment with similar spatial conditions.
63 Based on information from Agro Rural and the Peruvian Ministry of Agriculture.

In order to avoid these side-effects, an intelligent and measured approach is required, with an emphasis on indigenous species. The following pages describe the biological and economic benefits and risks of various commonly planted species.[63] →fig. 35-36

TREE PROPERTIES CHART

Data: folders and illustrated booklets published by the Peruvian Ministry of Agriculture (Ministerio de Agricultura, 1998)

PROPERTIES

- N — native species
- ✳ — tolerates extreme cold
- ☀ — tolerates drought
- ▲ — tolerates rocky soil and slopes
- ≡ — tolerates flooding
- ↑ — rapid growth

#	species	alt. (m)	N	✳	☀	▲	≡	↑	notes
1	Agave (*Agave americana*)	0–3500	•			•			Originally from Central America, this species is well distributed in the Andean region. The plant flowers from May to June and carries fruit from August to September.
2	Aliso (*Alnus Jorullensis*)	1200–3800	•			•		•	This tree of 10 to 15 meters high is distributed widely in the Peruvian Highlands. The tree has potential for agroforestry in the Andean region due to its rapid growth.
3	Casuarina (*Casuarina cunninghamiana*)	0–2200			•			•	This large tree can grow up to 15 meters or higher. Its appearance is similar to pines. Originally the tree comes from North-East Australia.
4	Cedro de altura (*Cedrela angustifolia*)	2800–3500	•	•		•			This large, leafy tree is endangered, with only some isolated individual specimens remaining in the region. It requires good soil and an ample amount of water.
5	Colle (*Buddleja coriacea*)	3400–4500	•			•			Colle varies from a 2 meter high bush to an 8 meter high small tree. It requires a deep soil, but tolerates stones. It is often planted at the borders of fields and pastures.
6	Eucalipto (*Eucalyptus globulus*)	2800–3500			•	•		•	Although not indigenous, Eucalipto is perhaps the most common large tree in the highlands. It thrives on difficult terrain, but extracts lots of water and nutrients from the soil.
7	Tara (*Tara spinosa*)	0–3000	•		•	•			This shrub grows to a height of 2–3 meters, and can be found everywhere in Peru. It is able to adapt to any kind of soil.
8	Tuna (*Opuntia ficus-indica*)	0–3000	•	•	•	•			This cactus can be found in both the coastal and highland areas of Peru. It grows up to 5 meters in height, and flourishes even on dry, low quality soils.
9	Queñua (*Polylepis incana*)	2800–5000	•	•		•			Queñua grows 4 to 10 meters high. Like other species of the genus, it has dense foliage, an irregular trunk, and flaking, multi-layered bark which protects from cold and sun.
10	Quinua (*Polylepis racemosa*)	2800–4000	•	•		•		•	A fast-growing, small tree, of the same genus as the Queñua.
11	Sauce (*Salix humboldtiana*)	100–3000	•				•	•	This tree attains a height of 12 meters or more and is often located at channel borders or close to agricultural land. It needs deep soil and humidity, but also tolerates rocky soil.
12	Sauco (*Sambucus peruviana*)	2300–3500	•			•			Sauco grows up to a height of 4 meters, and has a dense, pendular foliage. It prefers loose soil, although it can tolerate some rocks, and is naturally found along riverbanks.
13	Molle (*Schinus molle*)	200–3200	•		•		•	•	This 5 meter high tree has long leaves and clusters of red and pink berries. It prefers a loose, deep soil. Molle can adapt to zones with seasonal inundations.
14	Retama (*Spartium junceum*)	0–3500			•			•	This shrub grows to a height of 2 meters, with fragrant, yellow flowers. Originally native to the Mediterranean, it has long since been established in the Andes.

APPLICATIONS

- 🪵 high quality construction wood
- 🔥 high quality firewood
- 🌱 easily cultivated
- 🍴 nutritional e.g. fruit
- ✄ suitable as fodder
- 💧 tanines and dyeing products
- ✚ medicinal uses
- ∴ natural ground fertilizer
- ↑ provides shadow
- ⇒ suitable to retain soil

Constr. wood	Firewood	Cultivated	Nutritional	Fodder	Tanines/dye	Medicinal	Fertilizer	Shadow	Retain soil	Description
		•			•	•			•	Agave is harvested for many purposes, including making soap, extracting medicine and distilling alcoholic beverages. It is often used to stabilize steep slopes and gullies.
•		•	•	•	•	•	•			Aliso provides high quality timber and cellulose for paper. The bark can be used to produce tannins for leather. Various extracts of the tree are used as an antidote to rheumatism, arthritis and colds.
•	•					•			•	The wood of the Casuarina is of good quality and can also be used as firewood. Its deep roots retain soil and can prevent landslides.
•					•	•		•		The leaves of the Cedro de altura give off a bright brown colour often used to dye textile. In traditional medicine, components of the tree are used to treat hepatitis and liver problems.
•	•				•	•		•	•	Timber from the Colle is well-suited to construction works. An infusion of its flowers produces a yellow dye for the local textile industry. Its dense foliage provides shadow and shields against the wind.
•	•	•								The wood of Eucaliptus is fast-growing, straight, and has good characteristics for use in construction. It is easy to cultivate.
	•				•	•				The fruits of the Tara are a source of excellent tannins for the treatment of leather. The shrub begins to produce after about 3 years, and can supply 30 to 40 kg of fruit per year. The seed pods have medicinal uses.
			•		•	•			•	A mature Tuna plant can produce 200 edible fruits a year. The plant is a host for the cochineal parasite, which can be harvested to produce a crimson dye highly sought-after in the food and cosmetic industries.
•	•				•	•				Queñua wood has a high resistance and durability. Its foliage can produce a clear brown dye. Infusions of the leaves are used to treat tonsilitis, inflammations and colds.
•	•				•	•				Because of its speed of growth and resistance to rot, the (fire-)wood of the Quinua is greatly appreciated. The tree is often used for its ornamental value, due to its fuzzy leaves.
•					•	•		•		The wood of the Sauce is used for fabrication of doors and windows. The tree also has many medicinal uses: as an astringent, analgesic, anti-flu, anti-diarrheal, and anti-inflammatory.
•			•			•				Sauco wood is hard and durable. After 4 to 5 years, the tree starts to produce sweet fruits which are often used to make jams. Its leaves and flowers are considered a treatment for inflammations and rheumatism.
			•		•	•	•			This fast-growing tree is often used as a living agricultural fence. The leaves give off a terpentine scent when crushed, which repels insects. Its fruit is the basis of *chicha de molle*, a traditional ceremonial drink.
					•	•			•	Retama grows quickly and can be directly sown, making it suitable to protect against soil erosion along steep slopes and channel edges. The plant is often used ornamentally.

Urban terracing

This 'preparing of the ground' through irrigation, terracing and planting is equally relevant in contemporary urban situations. As the periphery of Ayacucho expands outwards, it leaves behind the flat, river-adjacent terrain where it was founded, ascending or descending the surrounding steep, dry slopes. To render these slopes inhabitable, they are likewise terraced. However, in contrast to agricultural land, the soon-to-be urban sites are often clear-cut, the topsoil is scraped from the bedrock, and much larger terraces are created: an aspired condition of placelessness[64] from which to start construction. →fig. 37-39

[64] To paraphrase Kenneth Frampton.

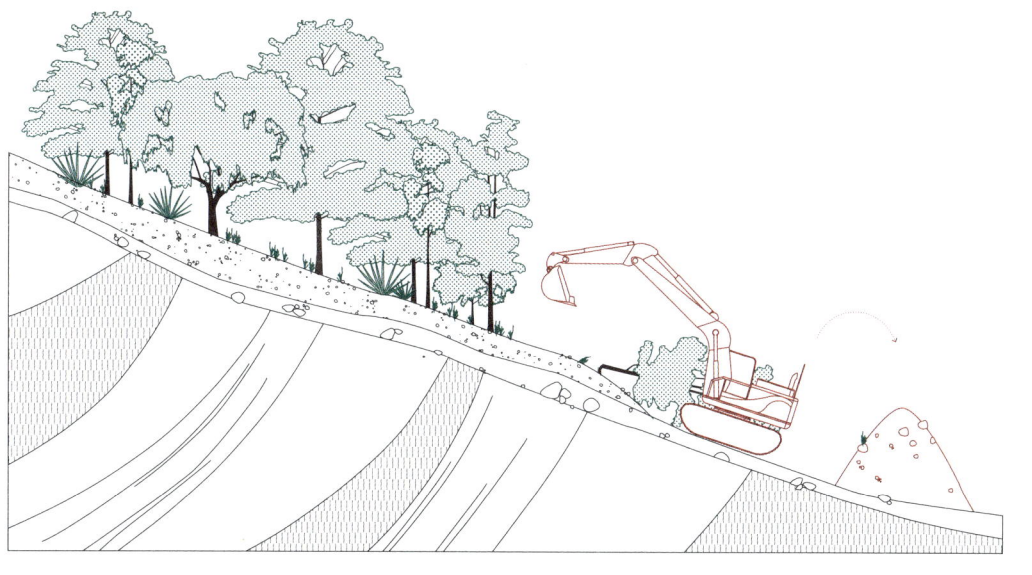

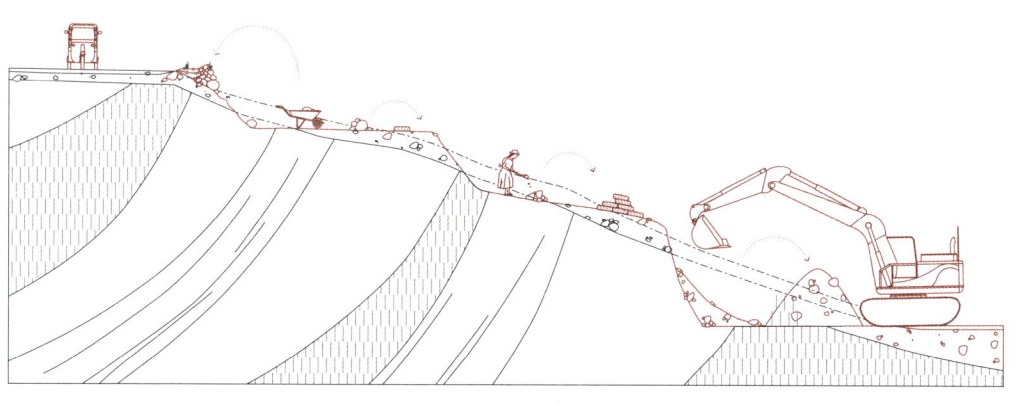

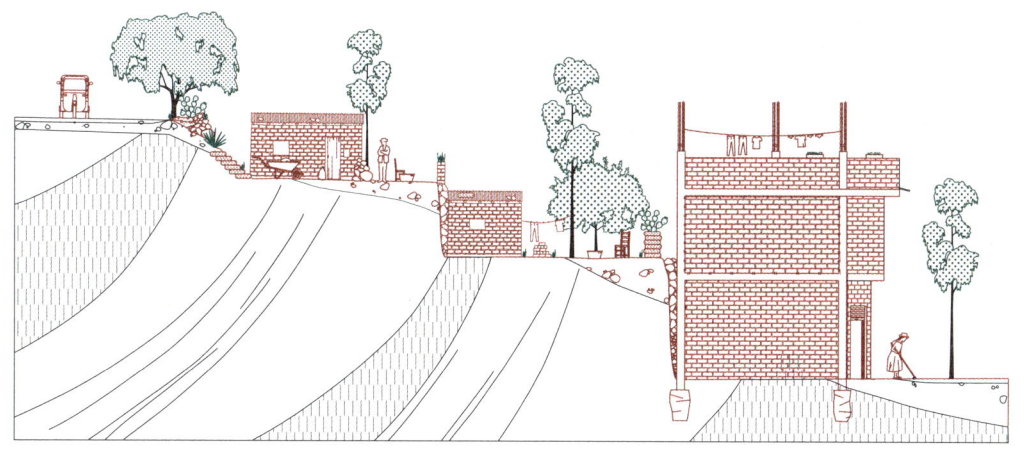

URBAN ANDES — PARALLEL NARRATIVES FOR CITY AND BASIN

This development goal fundamentally changes the behaviour of precipitation and surface runoff. Without topsoil, local infiltration is greatly reduced, and surface runoff amasses quickly as it courses downhill. Any remaining topsoil is soon pulled along by this flow, as it is no longer held in place by plant roots. The consequences are as described in a previous chapter: erosion, mudslides, and flooding. Current urban terracing practices would do well to learn from traditional techniques, which are more attentive to hydrology and soil conditions.

Despite this practice, it would not be correct to claim that no use is made of the excavated (top)soil. A portion of it is frequently used to make adobe bricks: the basic building blocks of the first iteration of most houses. This usage is not only a cost-efficient way to start construction. As discussed in the previous chapter, rapid consolidation of occupied terrain is essential in the context of land invasions, and the just-add-water on-site fabrication method of adobe bricks makes this possible.

65 Spanish for 'rustic house'.
66 Spanish for 'noble materials'. Both this term and the previous one arguably say more about how inhabitants view their standing within an urban environment than about the inherent quality of the constructions or materials themselves.

Incremental consolidation

As is typical in the Global South, housing in the new neighbourhoods of Ayacucho is usually constructed incrementally, as the number of occupants increases–not to mention their financial means. Often, the first act is the construction of a wall, marking and enclosing the limits of the purchased or self-appropriated plot. This is followed by the construction of a single-story dwelling, often comprising just one or two rooms. This type of adobe brick house is referred to as a *casa rustica*.[65] In a later stage, a new construction is started, using *materiales nobles*:[66] a concrete frame with an in-fill of fired bricks. Flat concrete roofs, with rebar protruding from the columns, define the skyline of Ayacucho and of many Andean cities like it. They lie in wait of future additional floors. Constructed correctly, these concrete-and-brick structures can rise several stories high while remaining resistant to earthquakes. →fig. 40-42

    In this way, the periphery gradually densifies over time. Extra square meters are used to house additional relatives, are converted into shops, or are turned into dorms for itinerant students or workers from surrounding villages.

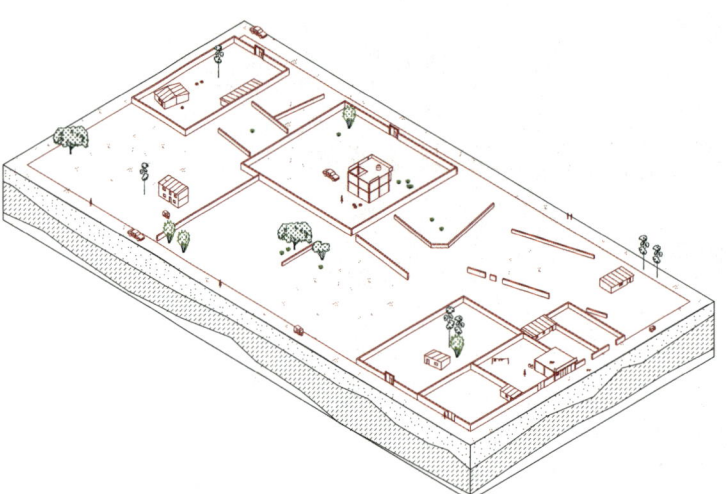

STAGE 1
Newly defined plots are enclosed by adobe walls. Construction of dwellings commences. Infrastructure is absent.

fig. 40

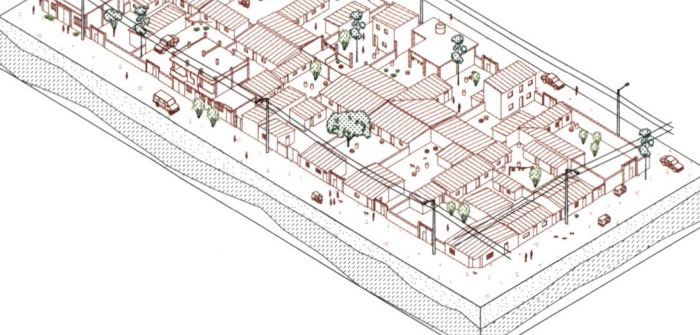

STAGE 2
The plots are occupied by single-story adobe houses. Services, for example electricity, begin to appear.

fig. 41

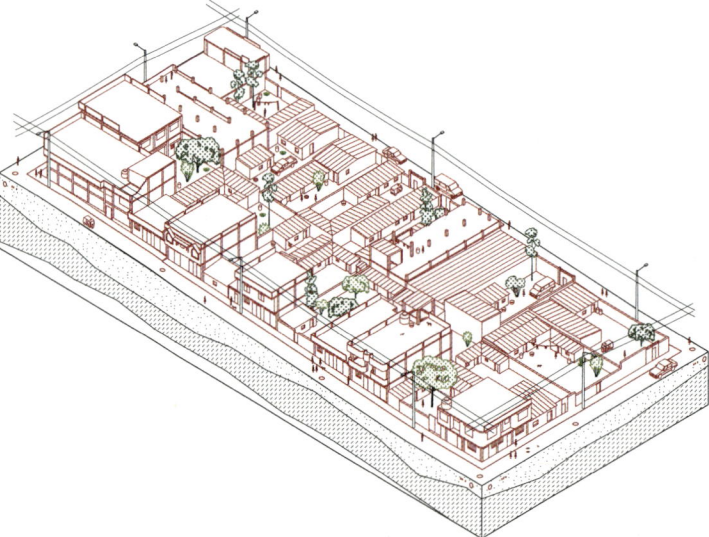

STAGE 3
The original dwellings are gradually replaced by multi-storied buildings made of concrete and bricks. Roads are paved, and a sewage system is installed.

fig. 42

Integration of incremental construction methods is a well-established strategy of progressive housing projects.[67] A further step would be to expand upon the material cycle of topsoil and adobe. Excavated topsoil not used for fabrication of adobe bricks could be implemented elsewhere to mitigate erosion and flooding. Discarded adobe bricks –for example those replaced by *materiales nobles*–could be reused in other constructions, or be reprocessed into fertile soil. As in the case of waste and rainwater recuperation, connecting and closing material flows can unlock much potential in the resource-deprived context of the Ayacucho periphery.

67 The most high-profile example perhaps being Quinta Monroy in Iquique, Chile, by ELEMENTAL.

REFERENCES

Alanya Arango, J. (1998). *Manual para Conservación de Suelos en Microcuencas Alto Andinas* [Manual for the Conservation of Soils in the Micro-basins of the High Andes]. Huancayo, Peru: Christian Impresores.

Bejar Romero, A., Pereyra Chavez, N. (2006). *La imagen de la ciudad de Ayacucho: tres coyunturas de expansión* [The image of the city of Ayacucho: three junctures of expansion]. *Dialogía, 1,* 159–183.

Buytaert, W., De Bièvre, B. (2012). Water for cities: The impact of climate change and demographic growth in the tropical Andes. *Water Resources Research, 48,* 8, 1–13.

Centro de Competencias del Agua (CCA). (2017). *Registr Metreolog Cachi.* Unpublished.

Chagnollaud, F. (2010). La andinización de la ciudad de Ayacucho: ¿la reconquista andina del espacio urbano? [The Andesization of the city of Ayacucho: the Andean reconquest of the urban space?]. *Pandora, 10,* 187–202.

Chagnollaud, F. (2016). *Urbanisation informelle par l'autogestion au Pérou* [Informal urbanization through self-management in Peru]. Paris, France: L'Harmattan.

Drenkhan, F., Carey, M., Huggel, C., Seidel, J., Oré, M. T. (2015). The changing water cycle: climatic and socioeconomic drivers of water-related changes in the Andes of Peru. *Wiley Interdisciplinary Reviews: Water, 2,* 6, 715–733.

Frampton, K. (1983). Towards a Critical Regionalism: Six points for an architecture of resistance. In *Anti-Aesthetic. Essays on Postmodern Culture* (pp. 16-30). Seattle, USA: Bay Press.

Gestión social del agua y del ambiente en Cuenca (GESAAM). (2016). *Gestión del agua y del ambiente en la micro cuenca del rio Cachi –diagnóstico 2015* [Management of water and environment in the micro-basin of the Cachi River–diagnostic 2015]. Lima, Peru: Sonimágenes del Perú.

Gobierno Regional de Ayacucho. (2006). *Proyecto Especial "Río Cachi"* [Special Project "Cachi River"]. https://studylib.es/doc/7510847/proyecto-especial-"r%C3%ADo-cachi"

Instituto Nacional de Estadística e Informática (INEI). (2017). *Compendio Estadístico Ayacucho 2017* [Statistical Compendium Ayacucho 2017]. Ayacucho, Peru: publisher unknown.

Lumbreras, L. (2006). *Un formativo sin cerámica y cerámica preformativa* [A Formative without pottery and pottery before Formative]. *Estudios Atacameños. Arqueología y Antropología Surandinas, 32,* 1–34.

Maldonado Fonkén, M. S. (2014). An introduction to the bofedales of the Peruvian High Andes. *Mires and Peat, 15,* 5, 1–13.

Ministerio de Agricultura. (1998). *Aprovechamiento Integral del Árbol* [Integral Use of Trees]. Lima, Peru: publisher unknown.

Ministerio de Agricultura. (1998). *Manejo de Plantaciones Forestales* [Forest Plantation Management]. Lima, Peru: publisher unknown.

Ministerio de Agricultura. (1998). *Manual de Plantaciones Forestales para la Sierra Peruana* [Forest Plantation Manual for the Peruvian Highlands]. Lima, Peru: publisher unknown.

Ministerio del Ambiente, Dirección General de Evaluación, Valoración y Financiamiento del Patrimonio Natural. (2015). *Mapa Nacional de Cobertura Vegetal–Memoria descriptiva* [National Land Cover Map–Descriptive Report]. Lima, Peru: MINAM.

Miranda Zambrano, G. A., Lindo Revilla, J., Santana Paucar, R. (2000). *Compartiendo los frutos de Pachamama* [Sharing the fruits of Pachamama]. In *Comida para el pensamiento–visiones antiguas y experiencias nuevas de la gente rural* [Food for thought–old visions and new experiences of rural people] (pp. 211-222). Cochabamba, Bolivia: Agruco/Compas.

Murra, J. V. (1974). *Los Limites y las Limitaciones del 'Archipelago Vertical' en los Andes* [The Limits and Limitations of the 'Vertical Archipelago' in the Andes]. In *Segundo Congreso Peruano del Hombre y la Cultura Andina, Trujillo, October 1974* (pp. 93-98). Trujillo, Peru: El Congreso.

Murra, J. V. (2017). Reciprocity and Redistribution in Andean Civilizations–The 1969 Lewis Henry Morgan Lectures. Chicago, USA: HAU Books.

Ochoa-Tocachi, B. F., Buytaert, W., De Bièvre, B., Célleri, R., Crespo, P., Villacís, M., Llerena, C. A., Acosta, L., Villazón, M., Guallpa, M., Gil-Ríos, J., Fuentes, P., Olaya, D., Viñas, P., Rojas, G., Arias, S. (2016). Impacts of land use on the hydrological response of tropical Andean catchments. *Hydrological Processes, 30,* 22, 4074-4089.

Pulgar Vidal, J. (1946). *Historia y geografía del Perú: Las ocho regiones naturales del Perú* [History and geography of Peru: The eight natural regions of Peru] (1st ed.). Lima, Peru: Universidad Nacional Mayor de San Marcos.

Servicio de Agua Potable y Alcantarillado de Ayacucho (SEDA). (2016). *Plan Estratégico Institucional 2016-2021* [Institutional Strategic Plan 2016-2021]. http://www.sedaayacucho.pe/archivos/258-plan-estratgico-institucional-pei-2016-2021-.pdf

Zapata Velasco, A., Pereyra Chávez, N., Rojas Rojas, R., Molina Richter, M. (2008). *Historia y cultura de Ayacucho* [History and culture of Ayacucho]. Lima, Peru: UNICEF, Instituto de Estudios Peruanos.

TABLE OF CONTENTS

A   FRAME

B   PROJECTION

3	FOREWORD
7	(RE)FRAMING THE URBAN ANDES
21	PARALLEL NARRATIVES FOR CITY AND BASIN
89	WORKSHOP #1 FROM BASIN TO CITY
103	THESIS EXPLORATIONS EMERGING NEIGHBOURHOODS
131	WORKSHOP #2 (RE)DEFINING AYACUCHO
153	AN ONLINE CONVERSATION

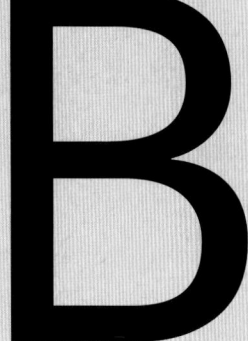

URBAN ANDES   PROJECTION

WORKSHOP #1

FROM BASIN TO CITY

AUGUST 2018

ADVISORS	BERNARDO AGUILAR LEON
	BRUNO DE MEULDER
	MARGARITA MACERA CARNERO
	WARD VERBAKEL
	BRAM WILLEMS
LOCAL SUPPORT TEAM	MARTÍN LEYVA
	CHRISTIAN NAKAIME
LECTURES BY	BERNARDO AGUILAR LEON
	BRUNO DE MEULDER
	TULIA GARCÍA LEÓN
	MARGARITA MACERA CARNERO
	WARD VERBAKEL
PARTICIPANTS	GENARO ALVA (PE)
	LOUISE BLANCQUAERT (BE)
	ELIANA CHUI (PE)
	ELISABETH DE CLERCQ (BE)
	LILIANA DELGADO (PE)
	GUSTAVO DIAZ (PE)
	MAGA GUANILO (PE)
	THOMAS HAWER (BE)
	WILLEM HUBRECHTS (BE)
	RAPHAEL KILPATRICK (AU)
	ROBYN MANSFIELD (AU)
	TAÍCIA MARQUES (BR)
	MAURICIO NUÑEZ (PE)
	KAREL VAN OORDT (PE)
	ANJA PIRJEVEC (SL)
	BRENDA QUIROZ (PE)
	CARLOS RAMOS (PE)
	RAMATLO TEBOGO (ZA)
	SIGRID VANGENEUGDEN (BE)
	DOUGLAS ZEVALLOS (PE)

FROM BASIN TO CITY   AUGUST 2018

"How can urbanization in the semi-arid landscape of the Andes occur without compromising the urban-rural hydrological balance of the territory?" The first international design workshop brought together local stakeholders and twenty students and young professionals over a ten-day period to investigate this key inquiry. Through intensive fieldwork and on-site discussions with local residents, community organizers, academics, and policy makers, the participants developed a multi-scalar, water urbanism-based vision. The research focussed on the relationship between basin and city and on several peripheral urban neighborhoods. These initial explorations were presented to and discussed with municipal partners at the end of the workshop.

CACHI BASIN
The deep section through the basin epitomizes the intricate relationships that exist between the headwaters and the urban lowlands. Understanding microclimate, as well as the different types of production that each ecological floor can host, is the basis for strong basin-wide links between developing social and spatial infrastructures. Water scarcity and rapid urban growth need to be addressed on a regional scale.

HEADWATERS
Due to climate change, the watershed is losing its glacial meltwater, requiring other water sources to upkeep the entire water chain supporting farming, dwelling, and production in general. As an alternative to large infrastructural works, local communities build and maintain low-tech retention ponds in the headwaters. *Qochas* and *bofedales* deliver usable water for food production and household use.

LOWLANDS
In the lowlands the current urbanization practices prioritize the construction and upgrading of mobility infrastructure, invading the productive hinterlands. Making such inroads challenges the landscape's capacity to provide the necessary resources to support urbanization. The workshop focuses on what we can learn from the headwater practices in urbanization processes that include water and landscape techniques.

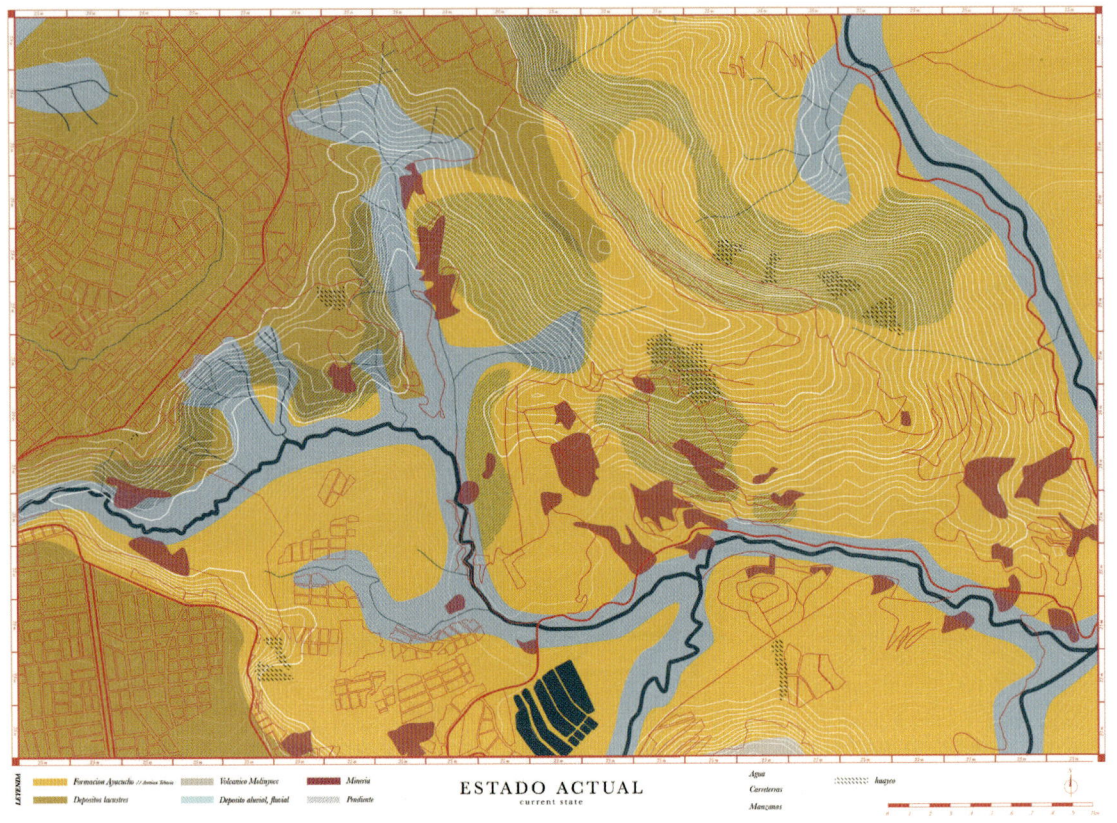

ESTADO ACTUAL
current state

MOLLEPATA AS AN EMERGING NEIGHBOURHOOD
In the semi-arid hills north of the city centre, the first signs of emerging neighbourhoods appear in the form of digging activities, drastically reshaping the landscape. By digging and piling earth, flat terraces are created with steep height differences between them. Stripped of its vegetation, the thin layer of fertile topsoil is even more prone to erosion and flash floods.

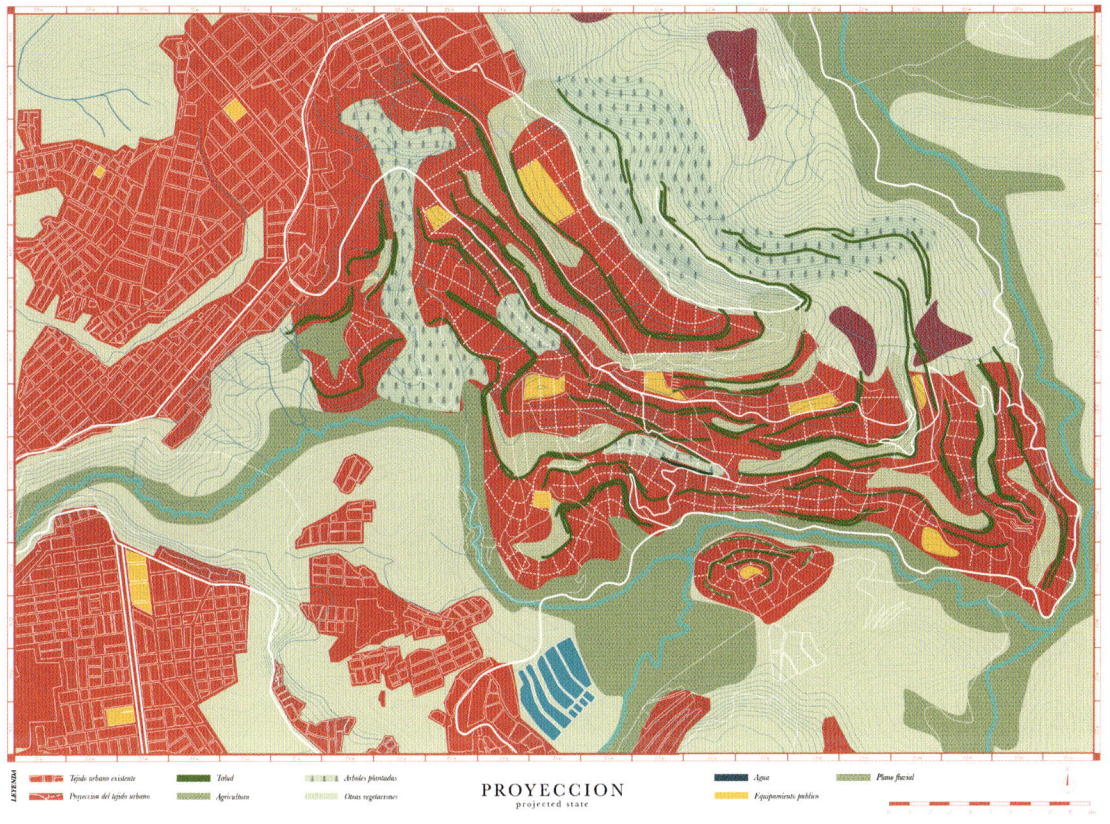

PROYECCION
projected state

DIGGING FOR FUTURES
An alternative settlement strategy takes the topography as its point of departure, specifically the dry creek beds featured throughout the site. Reimagined as water—and soil—retaining green corridors, they create the required conditions for small-scale agriculture, which in turn improves the food security of the adjacent communities. An other settlement pattern emerges, one that interweaves new housing with green ridges, berms, and water retention.

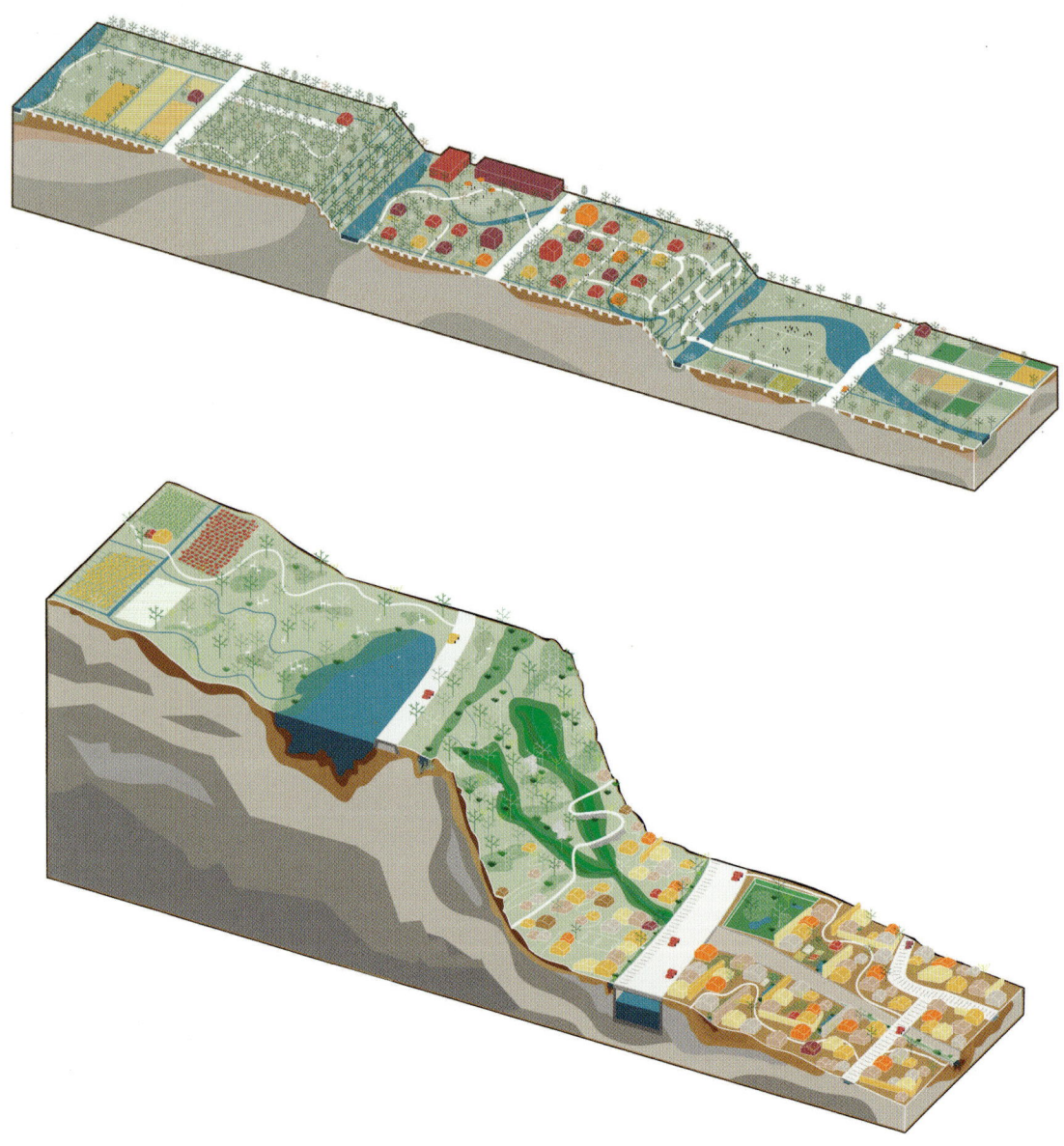

TERRACES AND FILTERS

By redirecting the ongoing terracing activity, the hillsides can become part of a soil improvement system that helps urban agriculture, water retention, and the overall quality of life. These filtering landscapes that benefit from the sloped conditions, are reimagined as a city scale buffer that slowly filters the surface runoff through the emerging neighbourhoods and vegetated flanks, allowing for the reuse and infiltration of seasonal rainwater. Large roads can become flash flood buffers; connecting roads at the top of the ridge introduce micro-dykes that control floodable parks; and steep streets on the slopes can integrate rain garden terraces.

PICOTA RIDGE STREETS
Where the city centre meets the Picota Ridge, steep streets climb up the flank. The simple pedestrian space is reimagined from a flash flood channel to a cascade of rain gardens, filtration ponds, and buffer plots in order to demonstrate what resilient water infrastructure can offer to public space on the smallest scale.

THESIS EXPLORATIONS:

EMERGING NEIGHBOURHOODS

2018-2019

AUTHORS	LOUISE BLANCQUAERT
	ELISABETH DE CLERCQ
	THOMAS HAWER
	WILLEM HUBRECHTS
	SIGRID VANGENEUGDEN
SUPERVISOR	WARD VERBAKEL
CO-SUPERVISOR	VIVIANA D'AURIA
ADVISORS	BRUNO DE MEULDER
	MARGARITA MACERA CARNERO

EMERGING NEIGHBOURHOODS   2018-2019

After attending the first Urban Andes workshop, five master's students from KU Leuven remained in the Ayacucho region to continue their fieldwork and stakeholder mapping, in dialogue with local NGOs and community representatives. Over the course of the following academic year, they further developed these initial explorations into a series of design research theses, closely guided by the OSA research group and design staff. Their project strategies for inclusive water management practices encompass various scales: landscape and urban systems, building typologies, construction methods, and cooperative models of land ownership. Their work was presented in Leuven at the VLIR-UOS funded Shout It Out event in 2018 and the sixth World Urbanism Seminar in 2019. It would also serve as the base for the second international workshop.

EMERGING NEIGHBOURHOODS
Five design projects were developed for and projected on the Ayacucho's emerging neighbourhoods and its surrounding landscape.

CHANGE OF COURSE   LOUISE BLANCQUAERT

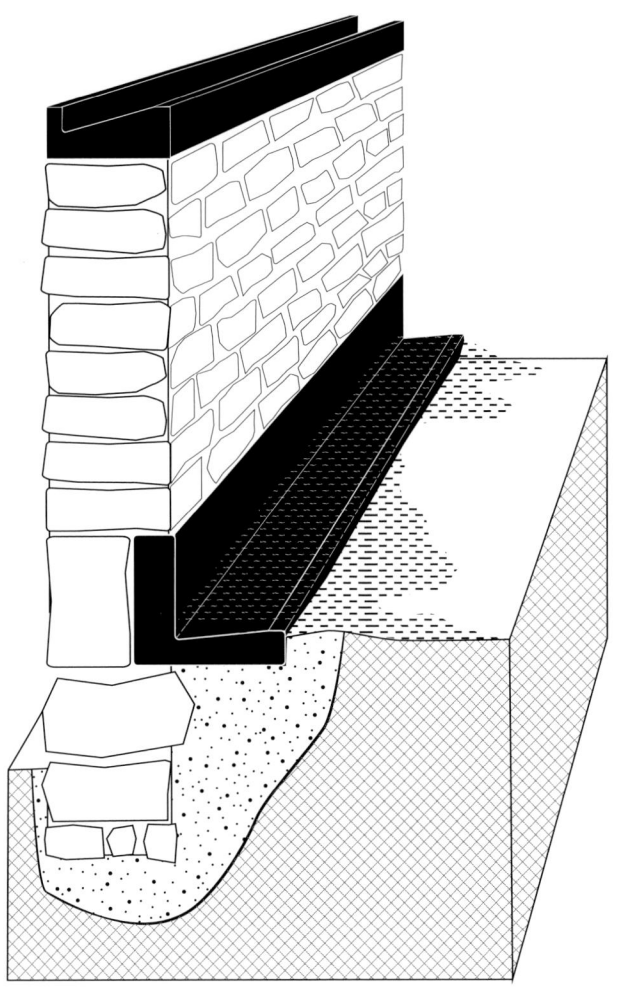

THE GUTTER AND THE WALL
Corresponding to the existing practice of self produced adobe bricks, a concrete gutter is introduced as a basic building element in emerging neighbourhoods. In this way, infrastructure for small-scale rainwater harvesting becomes interlaced with the built fabric. The contiguous implementation of both components is

1. A water garden in the street. Part of the street is overtaken by the water and vegetation.
2. A water passage in the block. Introducing a more private atmosphere in the street scape. A collective slow passage.
3. A water terrace. While the straight line of the street is kept, the height difference separates the terrace.

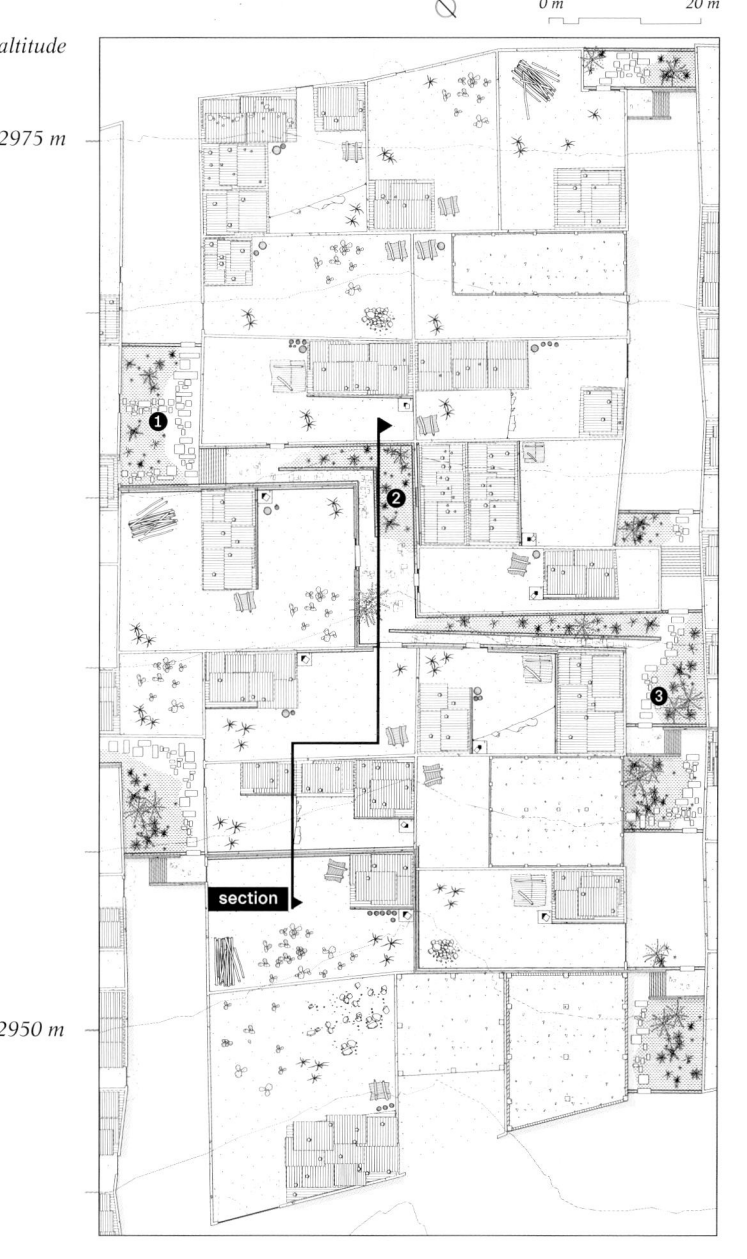

established through existing communal collaborative practices, known as *faena*. The incremental creation of a water network provides a water system that can halt the destructive vertical water flows along the Picota Ridge and create opportunities for storage and reuse of water within the urban fabric.

COMMUNAL SPACES
The redirected course of rainwater creates new spatialities in the neighbourhood. Households combine forces to invest in extra structures for optimal storage and (re-)use of the water, such as rain gardens and biofilters. The spaces occupied by these infrastructures break apart the strict grid of housing blocks and create secondary pathways. Whereas the existing streets often fail to contribute to the nuanced social life of the community, due to their steepness or to the dominance of motorised vehicles, these new pathways form small havens for communal life to prosper.

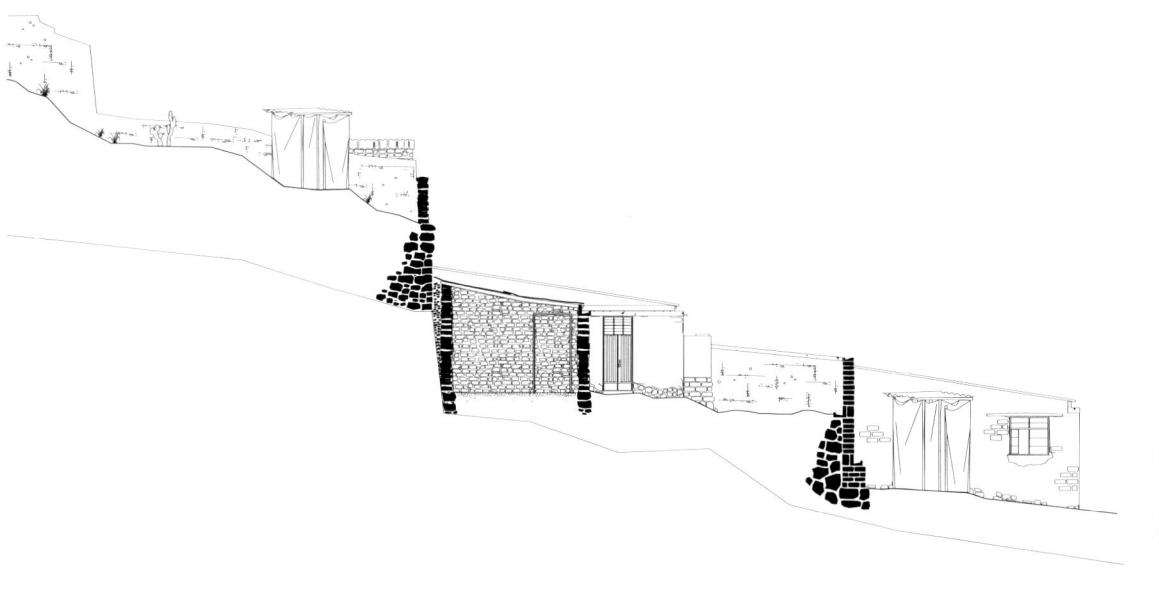

BUILDING BLOCKS   SIGRID VANGENEUGDEN

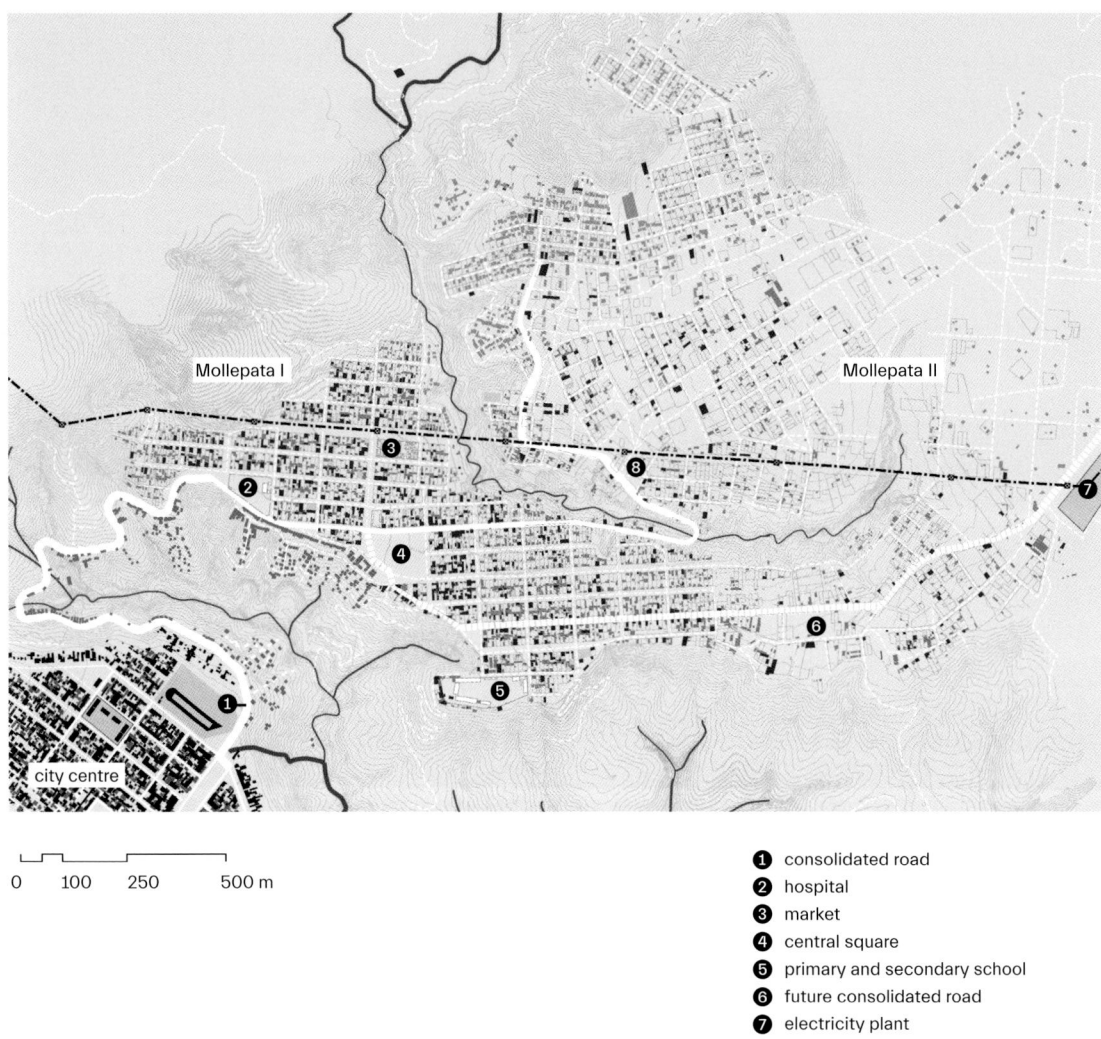

- ❶ consolidated road
- ❷ hospital
- ❸ market
- ❹ central square
- ❺ primary and secondary school
- ❻ future consolidated road
- ❼ electricity plant
- ❽ project site

CONSOLIDATION GRADIENT

Incremental housing construction in Ayacucho is characterized by a linear consumption of building materials: the adobe bricks used in the early phases of parcel consolidation, are later on discarded in favour of concrete and brick. Yet the varying degrees of consolidation of parcels within the neighbourhood of Mollepata represent an opportunity to create a local, circular construction system.

1. filtering incoming material flows
2. production of adobe blocks
3. oven for cement blocks
4. depot and (re)distribution centre
5. community house
6. grey water purification system with communal water tap
7. communal gardening and water storage
8. productive linear park

COOPERATIVE CONSTRUCTION

A construction cooperative, established in the centre of the neighbourhood, brings together all the material flows in order to orchestrate a circular process that eliminates the need for discarding previously used materials. Building upon the existing incremental building culture, this intervention invites the neighbourhood to work together, rekindling the spirit of Andean reciprocity in a contemporary context. Overtime, the coop can evolve alongside its surroundings, growing and shrinking, following the building needs of the inhabitants.

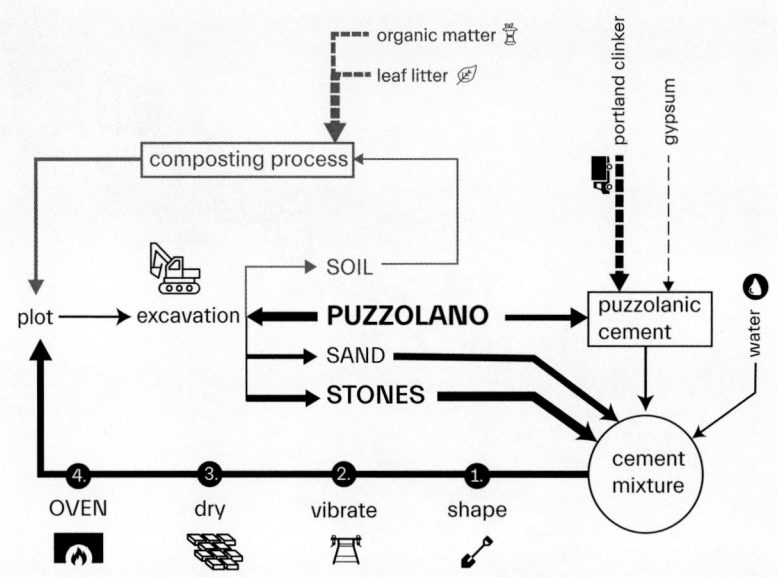

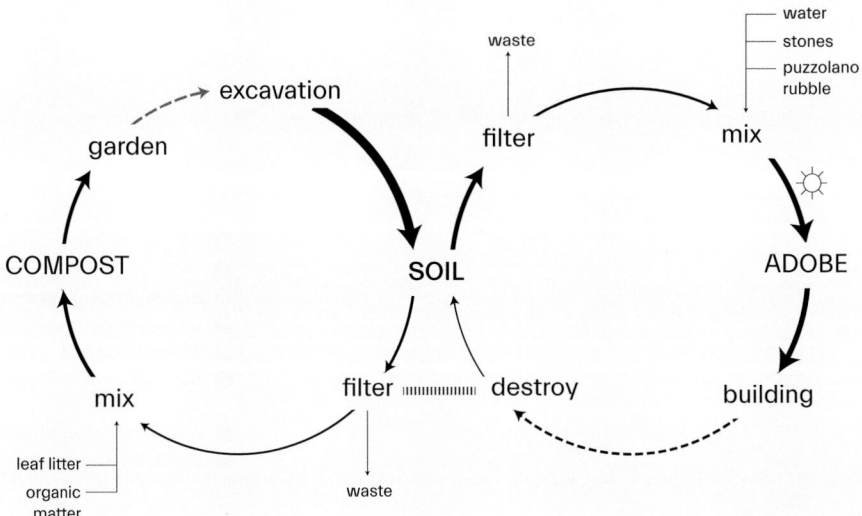

MATERIAL LOOPS
In the construction coop, discarded adobe elements are remade into new blocks, or are recycled into compost. Pozzolan, sand, and gravel extracted from excavated plots are used to make cement. Water, wood, and leaf litter are collected along the adjacent street. This street, situated in the *non aedificandi* zone below a high-voltage power line, is transformed into a productive, linear park, where native tree species are grown and grey water from the upper-lying neighbourhood is collected, filtered, and redistributed.

KNOWLEDGE CONSTRUCTION
In addition to building materials, the coop is also a source of knowledge and income. Maintained and managed by the local community, it is a place where skills are exchanged and revenue is redistributed.

OFF THE GRID   WILLEM HUBRECHTS

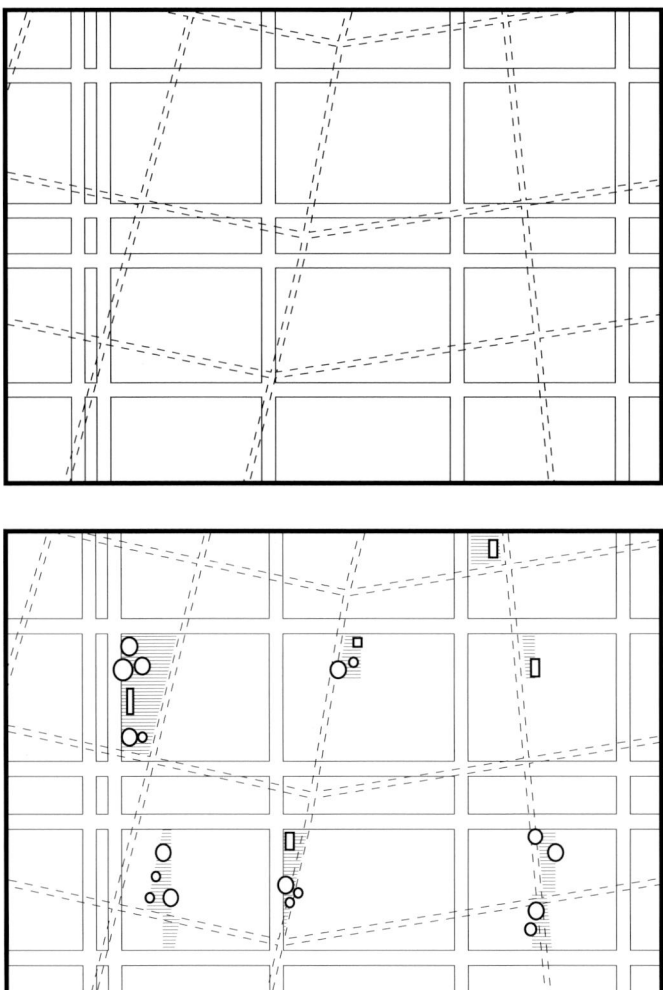

ACTIVATING THE 'IN-BETWEEN'
Irregularities in the grid dividing the plots of the Mollepata neighbourhood result in a series of triangular in-between spaces that are difficult sites for promoting individual housing projects. These leftover spaces can become sites for much needed water infrastructure on a collective scale. A network of water pockets buffers the rainwater and collects, filters, and stores the grey water coming from the households connected to it.

URBAN ANDES   THESIS EXPLORATIONS

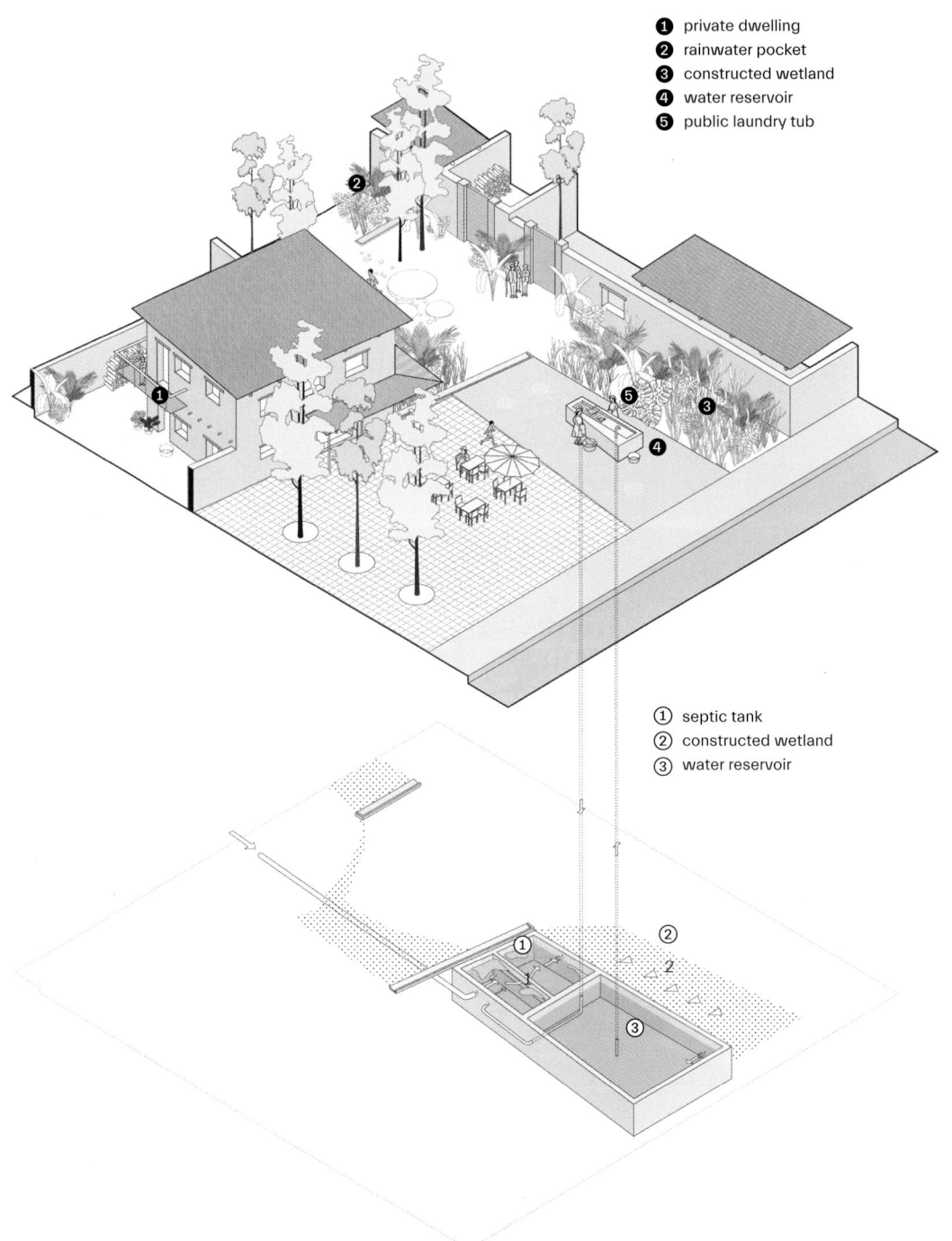

WATER INFRASTRUCTURE AS PUBLIC SPACE
At the end of alleys, (filtered) rainwater is collected in a larger water tank featuring a collective water tap in a small square. It not only provides clean water for local residents but is also a generous public gesture in a neighbourhood where qualitative spaces for informal encounters are scarce.

1. permeable stratum
2. perforated pipe
3. vegetation layer
4. pump
5. perforated coping stone

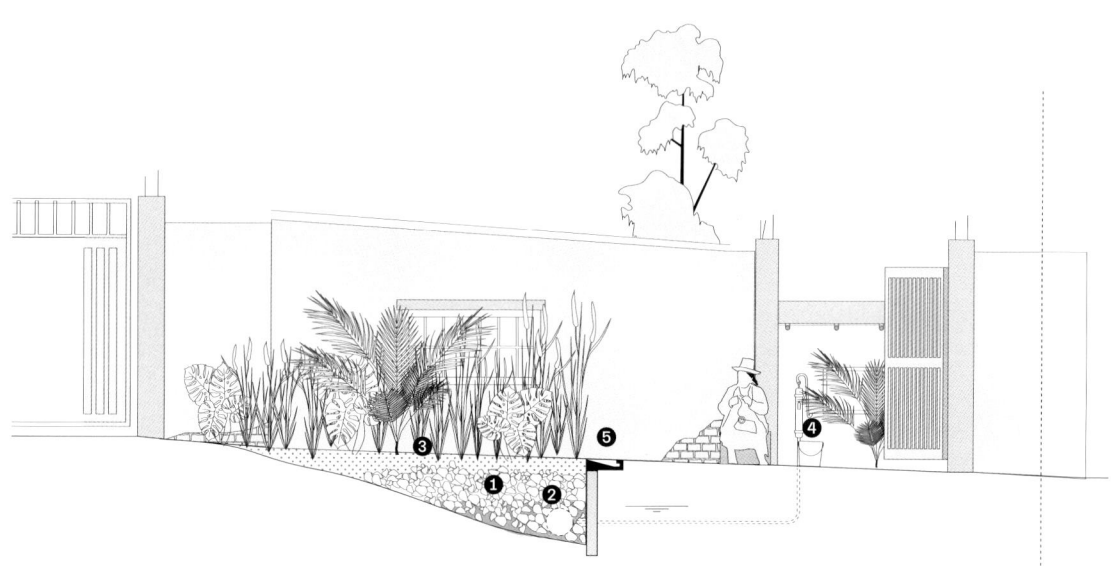

WATER POCKET
In order to bridge the critical weeks between the beginning of the rain season and the moment the headwater reaches the city, an infrastructure of water pockets can offer a buffer capacity. The rocky impermeable soil, in combination with gravel beds and a planted top layer of soil form the low-tech elements of an ingenious system of water pockets throughout the neighbourhood.

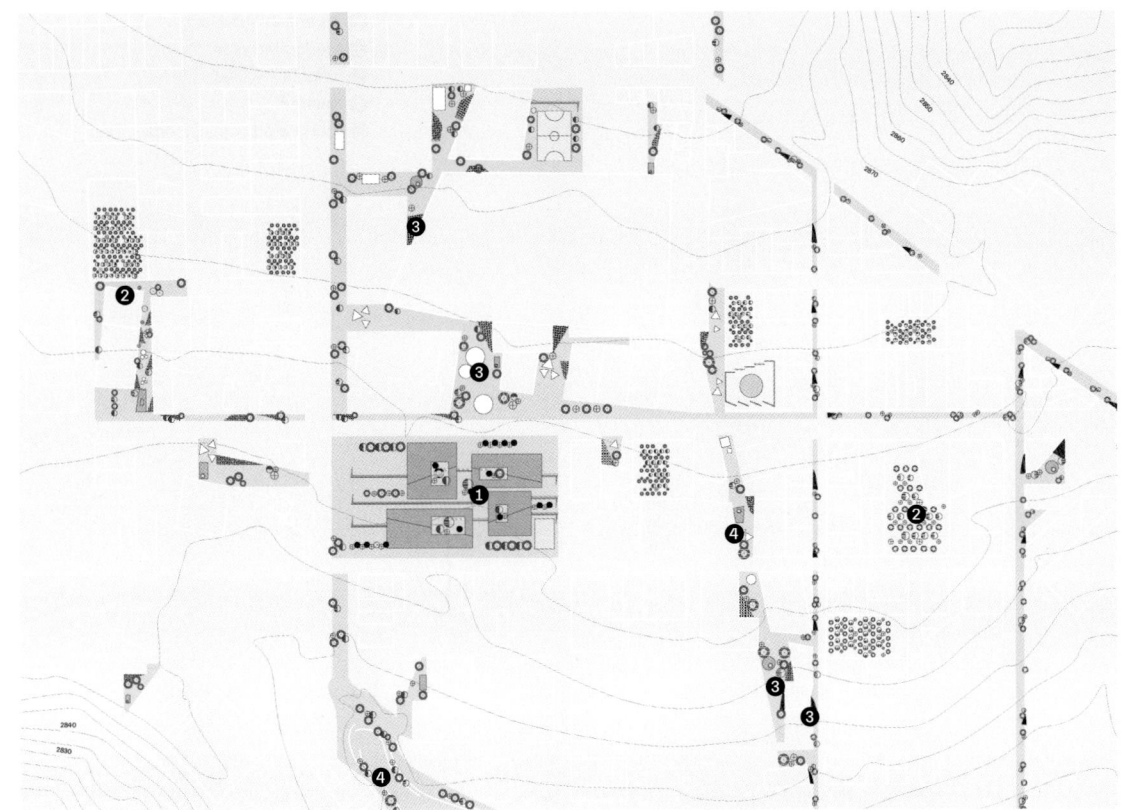

1. public patios
2. tree nursery
3. activated in-between space
4. water buffering streetscape

AN ALTERNATIVE NETWORK
These small-scale water infrastructures can be initiated by a group of neighbours in a local and informal setting. Together, these by-products of bottom-up land division projects form a connected public space system, consisting of passageways and pocket parks. This results in a secondary structure of green, car-free pathways enriching the original orthogonal grid that was laid out by the first settlers.

A LAZY SUNDAY AFTERNOON
Imagining public space and encounters around new water infrastructures that emerge throughout the neighbourhood. Woven in between the individual parcels, a water system that works as a backbone for the community, offering fresh water, a laundry facility, a moment to meet.

URBAN PLATFORMS — ELISABETH DE CLERCQ

A CITY ON SLOPES
Housing shortages in Ayacucho force new settlers to occupy the steep slopes of the urban periphery. These urban expansion practices, in which mountains are excavated for making terraces, cause erosion by disrupting soils, land cover, and ecosystems. The project proposes a renewed strategy to incrementally build neighbourhoods in this topographically challenging area, paying special attention to customary Andean techniques, neighbourhood emancipation, and proper water/soil management. At the heart of the new neighbourhood lies a soccer field which also serves as a large flat water reservoir.

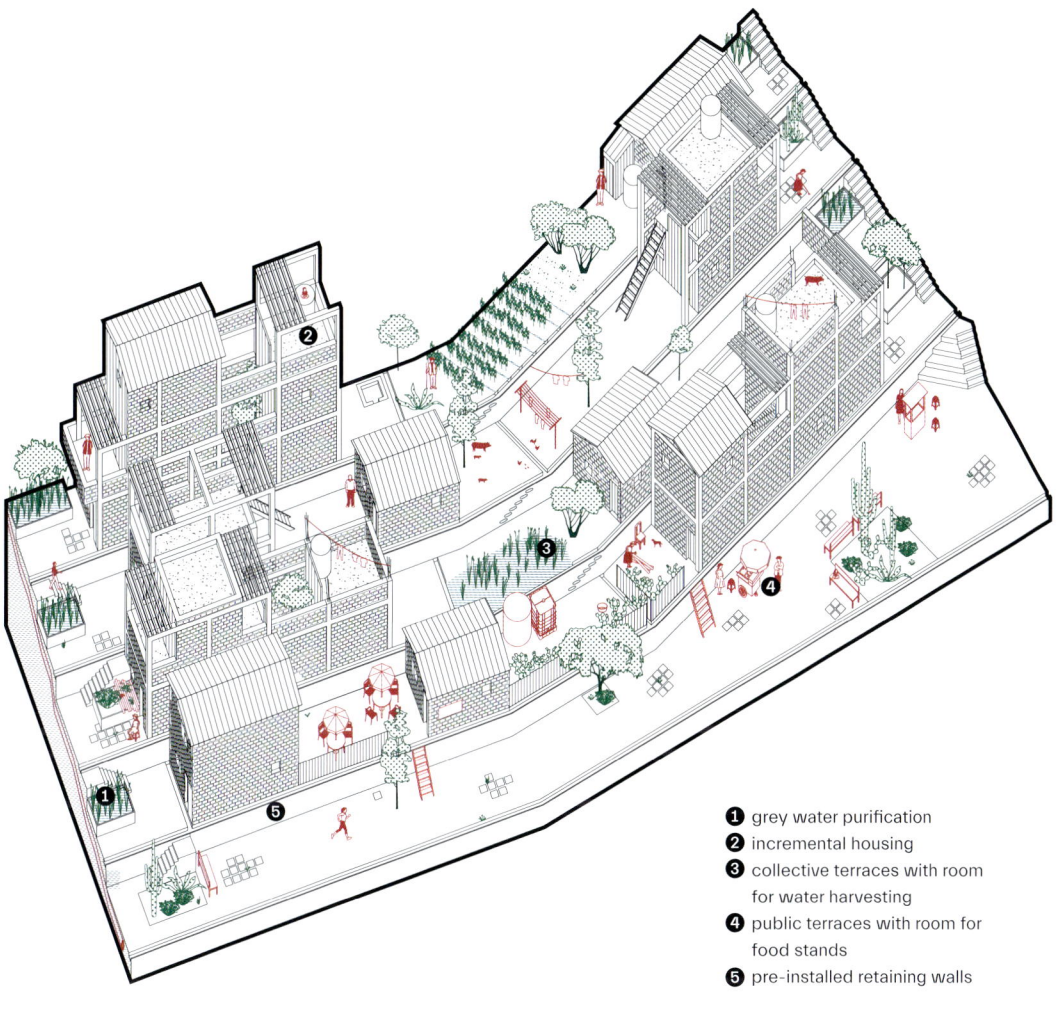

1. grey water purification
2. incremental housing
3. collective terraces with room for water harvesting
4. public terraces with room for food stands
5. pre-installed retaining walls

ANDENES AND COLLECTIVITY

Andenes are terraces dug into mountain slopes by Andean civilizations to facilitate agriculture while managing water and soil. The design strategy draws inspiration from this ancient engineering technique to provide new urban settlers a solid foundation, as well as to conduct water without eroding fertile soil. As in ancient times, the *andenes* can be collectively maintained. They provide the basis for retaining water, cultivating vegetables, keeping livestock, or accommodating communal facilities.

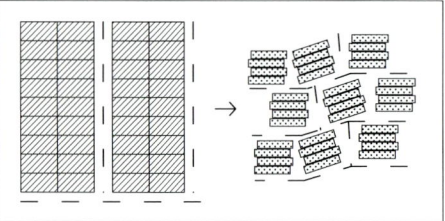

1. current parcellation practice
2. urban platforms
3. pedestrian bridge/erosion dam
4. natural water corridor
5. soccer field/water buffer
6. mobility hub
7. common terraces

PLATFORM(S) FOR GROWTH

The terraces do not intervene at the level of the actual construction of the individual house, which settlers are capable of organizing on their own. Rather, the terraces prefigure a socially and ecologically more resilient form for the neighbourhood— precisely the scale that is often neglected during the initial drive for settlement consolidation. They are platforms for the incremental growth of robust and resilient communities.

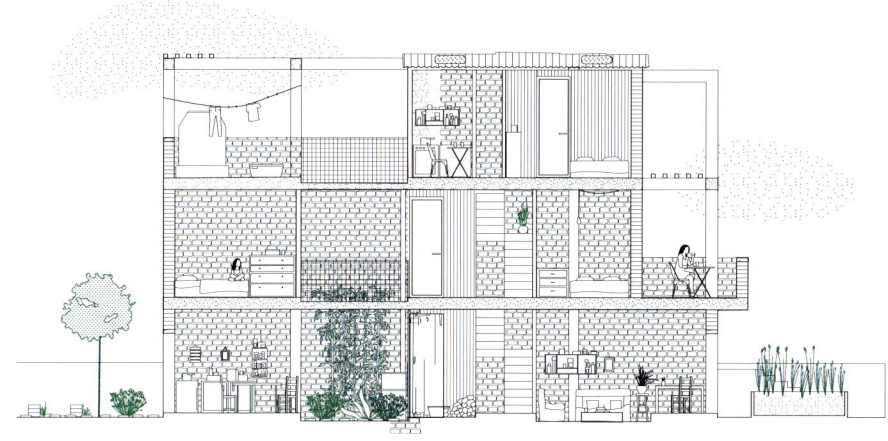

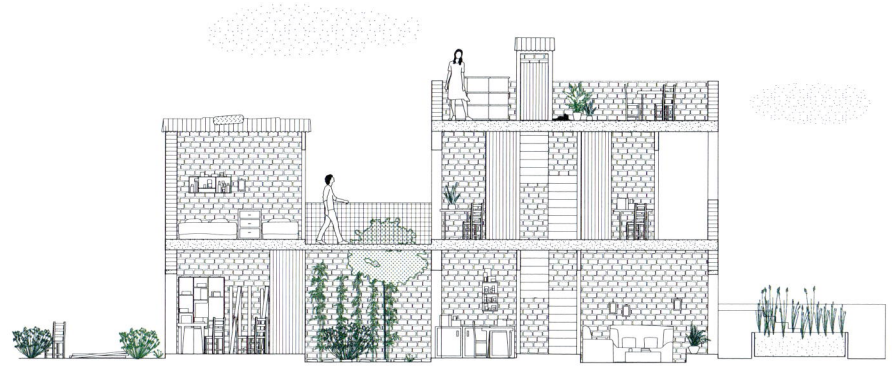

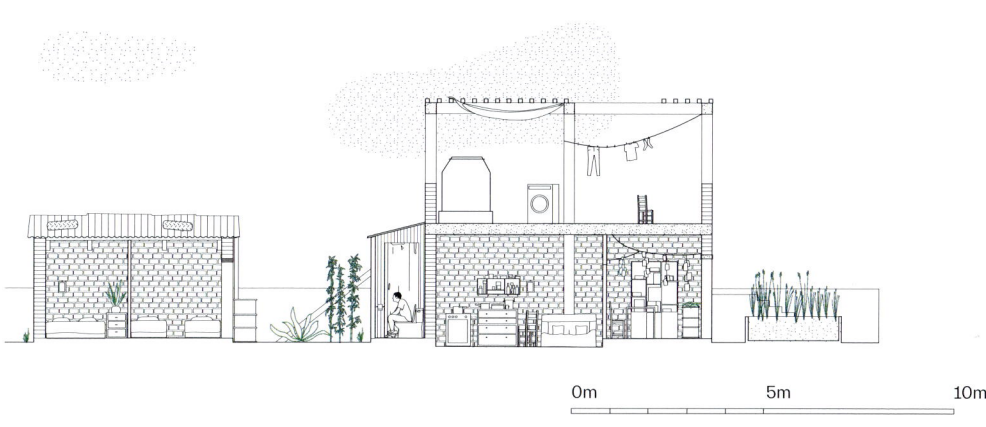

0m 5m 10m

HOUSING MODULES
This series of sections illustrates how different housing typologies can evolve from the platforms and retaining walls. They vary from multi-family and stacked housing projects to work-live units that can include small shops, home offices, or light manufacturing activities such as woodworking.

INTER-ACTION   THOMAS HAWER

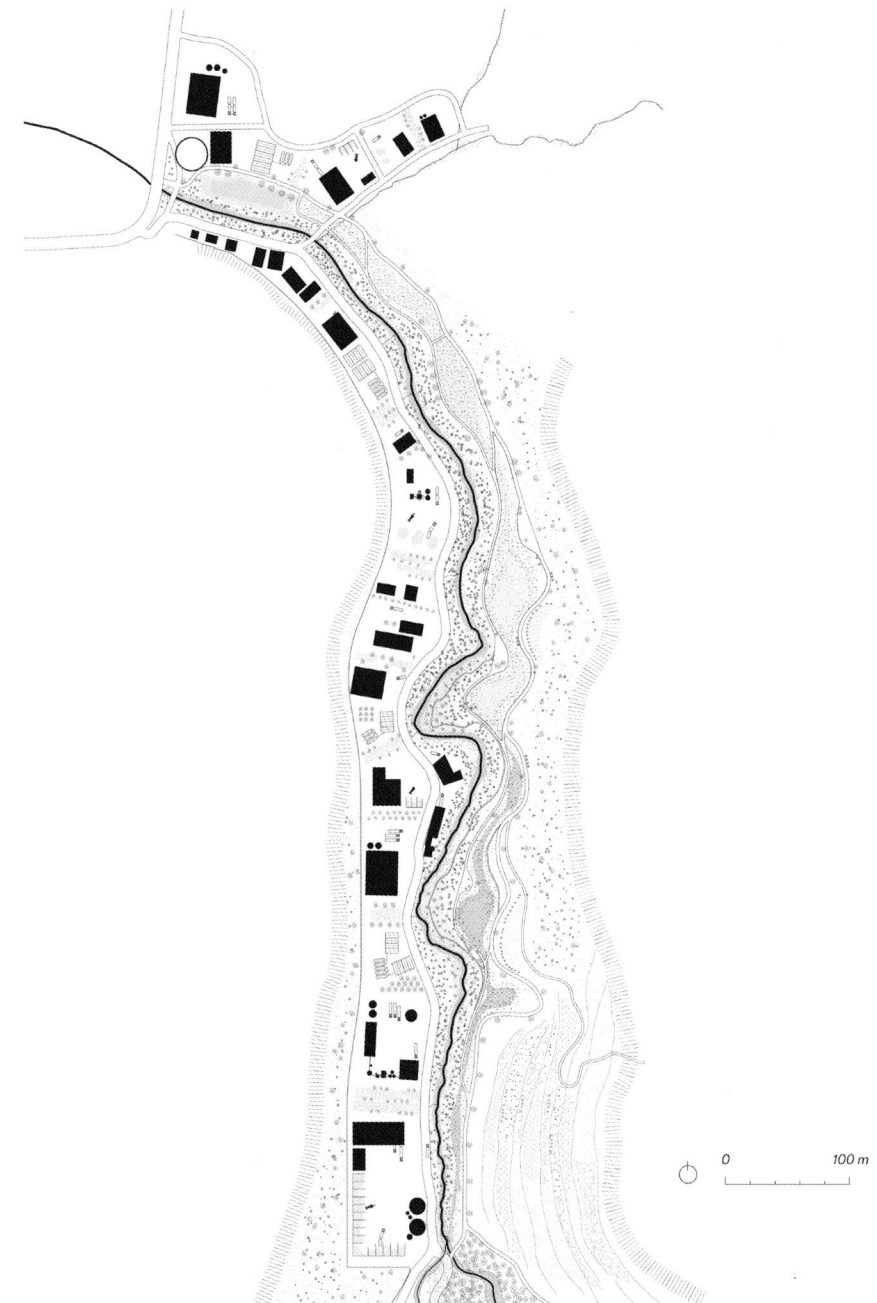

THE CONTEMPORARY VERTICAL ARCHIPELAGO
Looking at the transformation of a semi-urbanized valley north of the city, this project focuses on the potential of the productive landscape. In an attempt to restore the imbalances created by the superposition of infrastructures, water scarcity and soil, overexploitation, and in order to regain a more meaningful role within the region, the valley is reimagined as interconnected ecological floors. The traditional Andean socio-economic structure is taken as an alternative model, one capable of melding productivity, settlement patterns, and landscape logics.

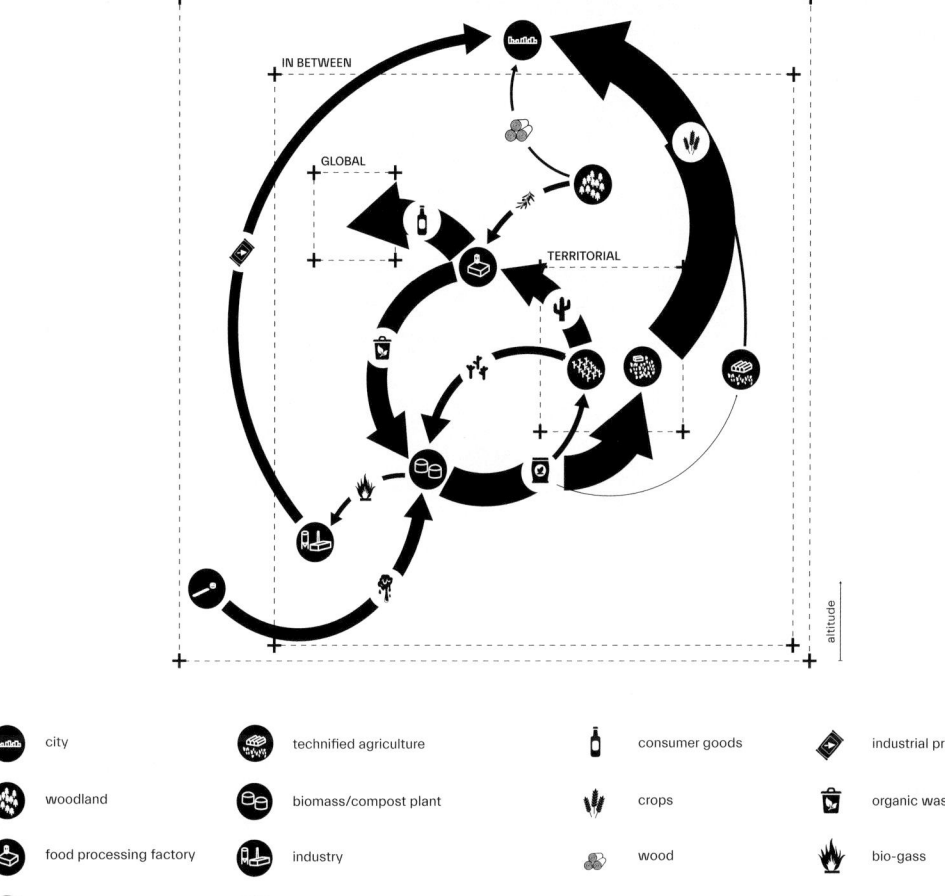

LOCAL ADDED VALUE

Although many locally produced resources are consumed as raw products within the region of Ayacucho, the significant added value resulting from the further processing of these resources is generally realized elsewhere. By exploring the possibilities of dry agriculture in relation to a food-processing factory, the valley could showcase the assets of a secondary processing economy. The phased development of the factory and its auxiliary network produces a series of urban and hydraulic patterns. Responding to both the gridiron urban morphology and to the irregular topography of the site, the project offers an example of how a productive entity can become the locus of communal activities.

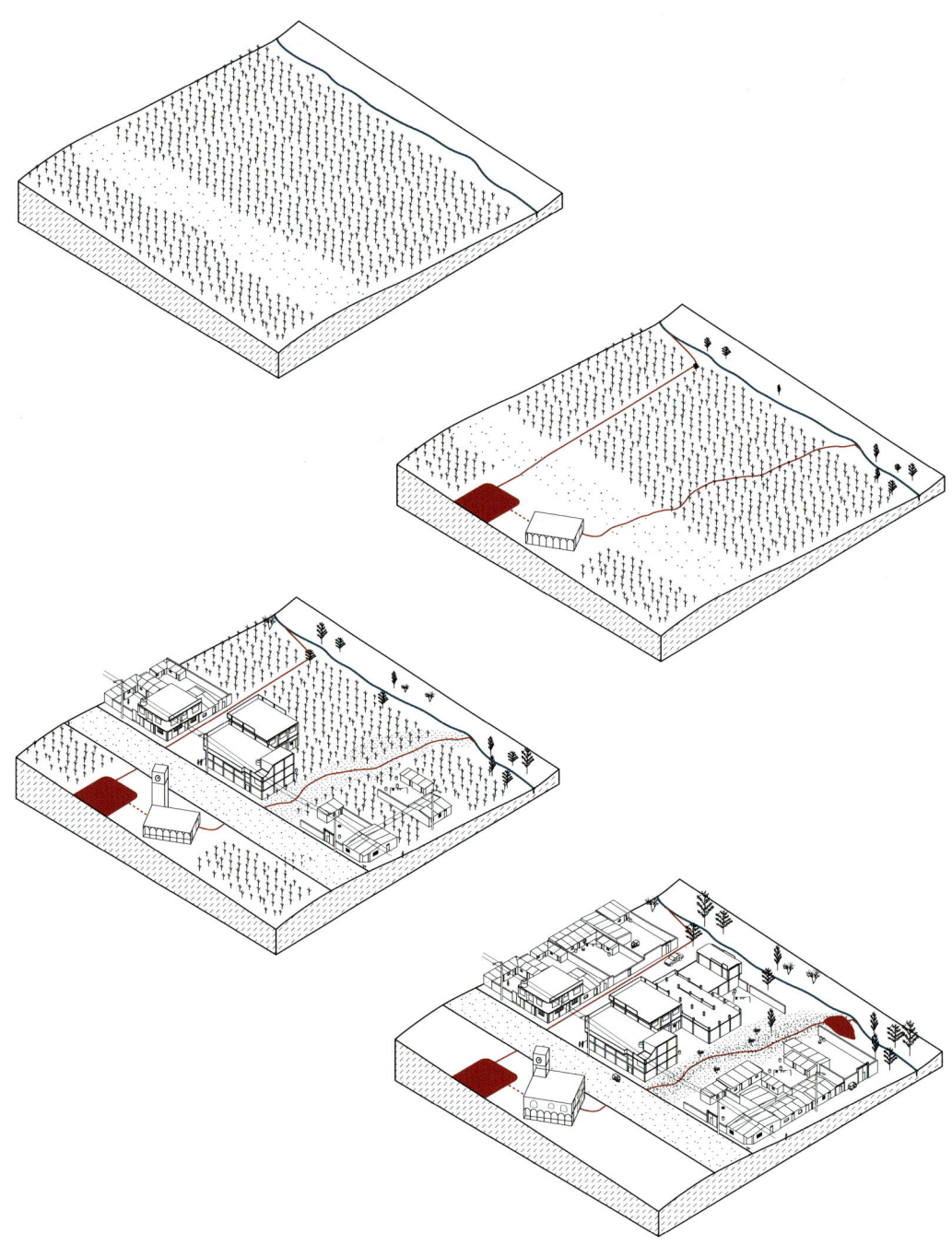

HYDRO-INDUSTRIAL SYMBIOSIS
The production complex is combined with a natural water treatment plant, anticipating the increased water demand of future production activities. A new urban/rural archipelago emerges: a combination of infrastructure, riparian biotopes, industry, and food production facilities through which water cycles in a closed, regenerative loop.

WORKSHOP #2

(RE)DEFINING AYACUCHO

AUGUST 2019

ADVISORS	BASIL DESCHEEMAEKER
	MONICA RIVERA MUÑOZ
	WARD VERBAKEL
	BRAM WILLEMS
LOCAL SUPPORT TEAM	VYERA DIANA CHIPANA MOLINA
	JUAN JOSE IPIÑA VEGA
	MARIA ÑOPE
	ROSANA VENTURA CAVERO
LECTURES BY	LOUISE BLANCQUAERT
	ELISABETH DE CLERCQ
	BASIL DESCHEEMAEKER
	TULIA GARCÍA LEÓN
	WILLEM HUBRECHTS
	TAÍCIA MARQUES
	WARD VERBAKEL
PARTICIPANTS	(PICOTA RIDGE)
	OSCAR BECERRA VARGAS (PE)
	LOUISE BLANCQUAERT (BE)
	RUSSELL HUAMÁN (PE)
	JONAS LENS (BE)
	SHAUNI MARCHAND (BE)
	CAROLINA ZEGARRA (PE)
	(MOLLEPATA HILL)
	WILLEM HUBRECHTS (BE)
	KARLO RAMIREZ RIVAS (PE)
	COURTNEY SPRIGG (US)
	NOEMÍ TOMAYLLA (PE)
	LOTTE VANSANT (BE)
	FLAVIO VILA SKRZYPEK (PE)
	(ALAMEDA VALLEY)
	LIESBETH BUYS (BE)
	ELISABETH DE CLERCQ (BE)
	JUAN JOSE IPIÑA VEGA (CL)
	CARLOS MORALES DÁVILA (PE)
	GIANINA PAUCAR (PE)
	ALINE VAN DRIESSCHE (BE)

Through an open call, eighteen Peruvian and international participants were selected to take part in the second design workshop. During this edition, focus shifted to the urban scale and to the potential of landscape urbanism strategies to imagine alternative futures for the city's expansion and consolidation. The design research proposals aim to investigate and reveal synergies relating to water scarcity, forms of land appropriation, public- and private-sector construction, bottom-up community development, and top-down municipal planning. The results were presented at the *Expo Ciudades y Comunidades Sostenibles en Perú*, which took place on the final day of the workshop.

THREE LANDSCAPE FIGURES
Three prospective landscape figures were defined as a starting point for the workshop, each representing a different relationship between city and basin: Alameda Valley, Picota Ridge, and Mollepata Hill. Each forms a laboratory for water-based strategies aiming to strengthen these figures and create a legible framework for individual design interventions. Two key sites per figure were then selected and further elaborated through precise design interventions.

A WATER-INCLUSIVE FUTURE FOR AYACUCHO

A triptych of collages imagines an Ayacucho that does not need to evolve against its landscape but that structures its urban expansion in accordance with underlying water logics. In the Alameda Valley, the river is celebrated for the central role it has and still should play in the development of the city. Picota Ridge is reimagined as an inhabited, sloped water retention park. Meanwhile, Mollepata Hill becomes an additional gateway to the city, welcoming new communities and economic activities.

ALAMEDA VALLEY

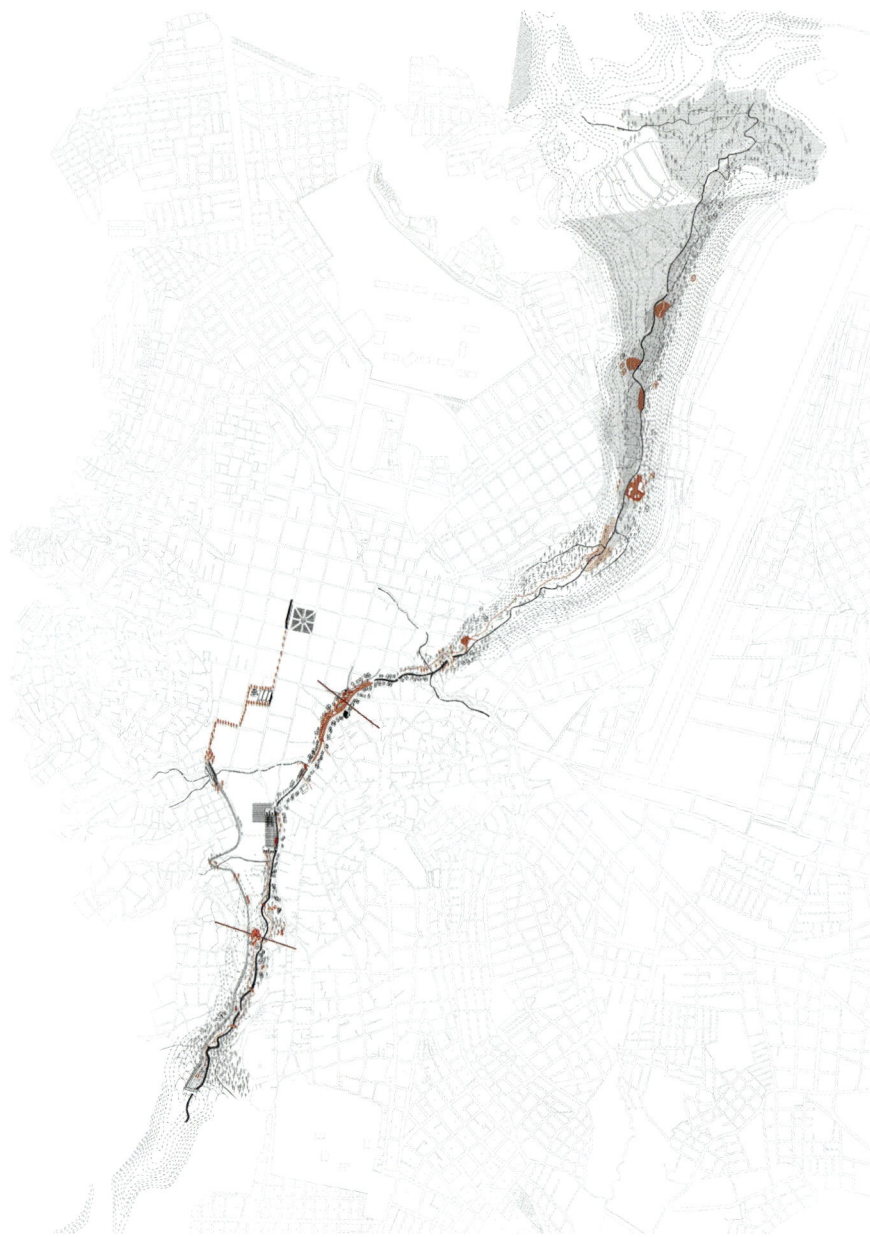

REMEMBERING THE RIVER
A series of design interventions is proposed over the length of the Alameda Valley's urbanized course. There is of course an emphasis on the reopening and renaturalization of the river in order to allow a more resilient river system, even in the urban core. The reactivation of historic elements as part of a continuous water logic through the urban fabric is more locally specific: an aqueduct that once brought potable water to the *Plaza de Armas*; disused water channels; monumental bridges and fountains. At other locations, existing social and agricultural practices inform not only the potential programming of the spaces but also the methods of their realization.

TRANSFORMING MORASPAMPA
Three steps illustrate the potential transformation of Moraspampa, a peripheral neighbourhood lying upstream of the city centre. The short term focus is on accessibility to water: inhabitants are brought to the river via a network of stairs, and the river water is brought to the inhabitants by small channels. Interventions are low cost and executed through local initiative, according to the principles of *faena*. In the mid and long term, investment costs are upscaled through the involvement of municipal actors. A linear botanical garden safeguards the floodplain of the river, in addition to housing an installation to convert urban waste into compost. Sewage pipes in the streets divert grey and black water, keeping the Alameda clean. The valley protects the river.

PICOTA RIDGE

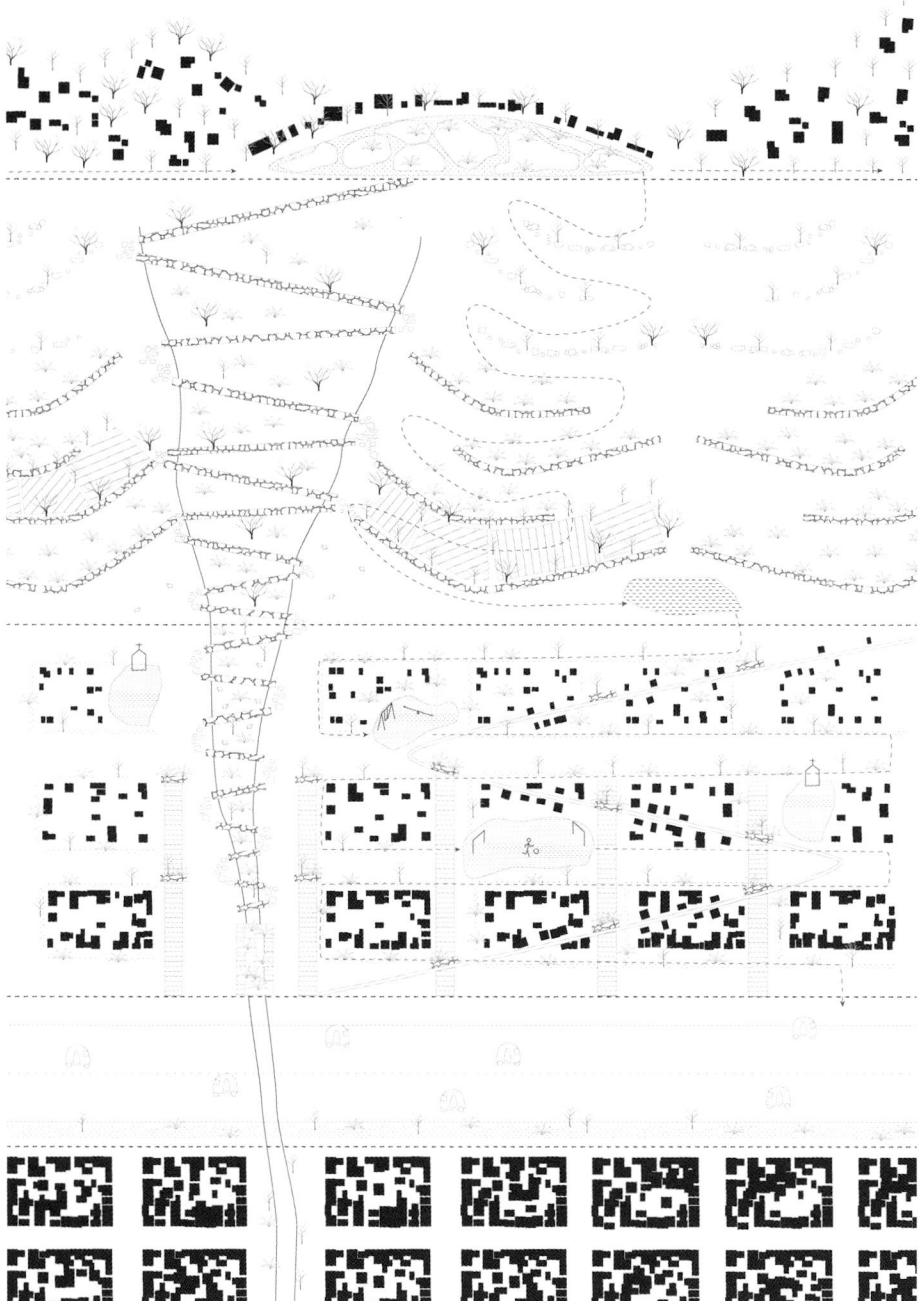

LIVING SLOPES
Excess surface runoff during rainfall regularly causes portions of Picota Ridge to collapse, perpetually threatening the city centre below. The proposed design addresses this risk by reimagining the entire slope as a green infrastructure that buffers, guides, collects, and purifies water, at the service of local communities. The unpredictable ridge becomes an inhabited and productive park on the scale of the city.

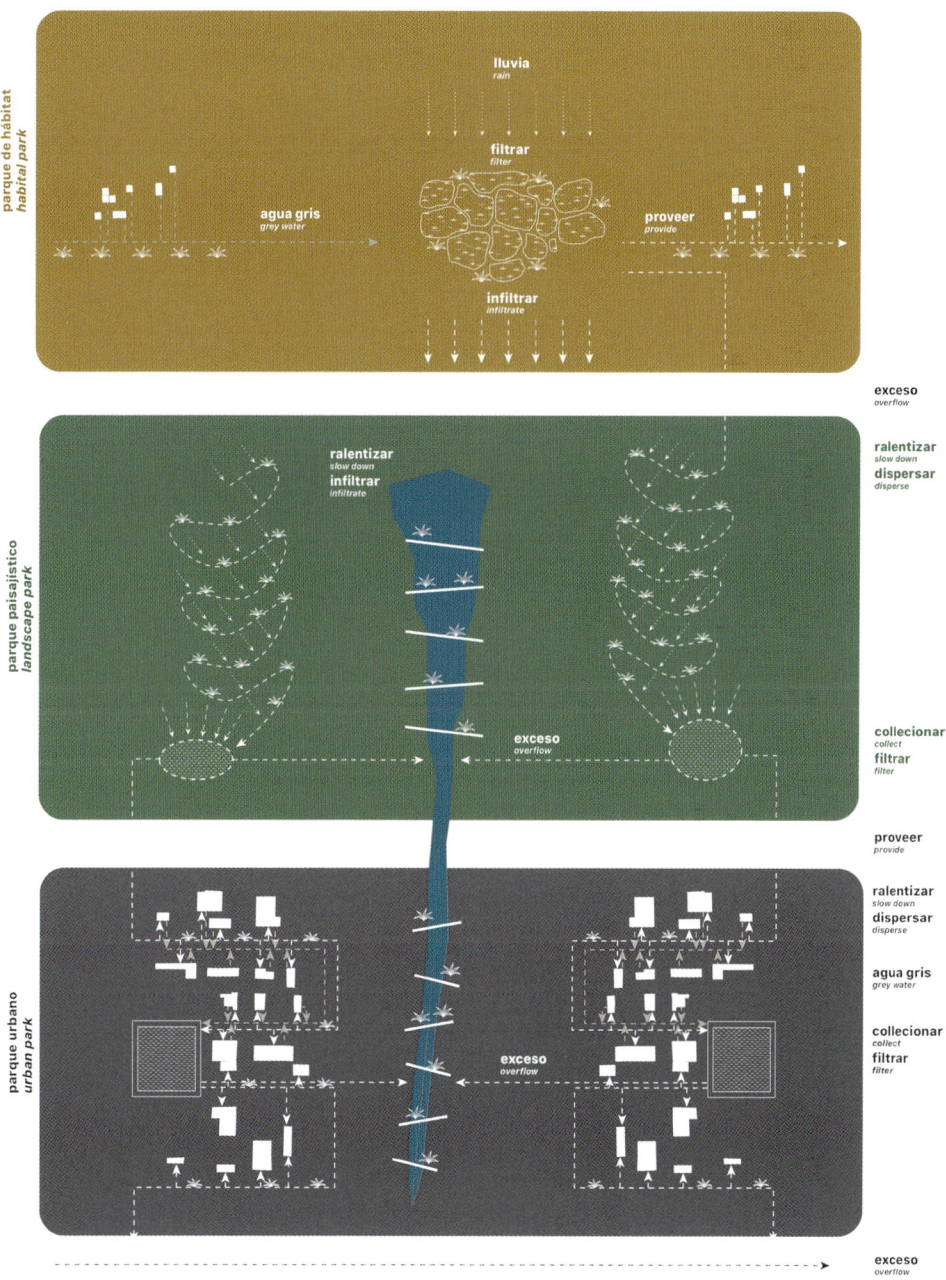

STRATIFIED STRATEGIES
Four typologies are defined, each requiring specific water management strategies: the plateau, natural slopes, urbanized slopes, and dry creeks. Within each typology, different degrees of urbanization are possible, ranging from public outdoor programmes to services and additional housing.

TYPOLOGIES
- plateau
- natural slopes
- urbanized slopes
- dry creeks

THE MICRO-BASIN AS CONNECTOR

A precise reading of the existing hydrological, vegetal and urban structures makes it possible to identify which typology can be applied to which zone. The ridge's micro-basins traverse these typologies, and it is on this scale that the different strategies are connected.

VEGETATION

··· native vegetation

··· reforestation

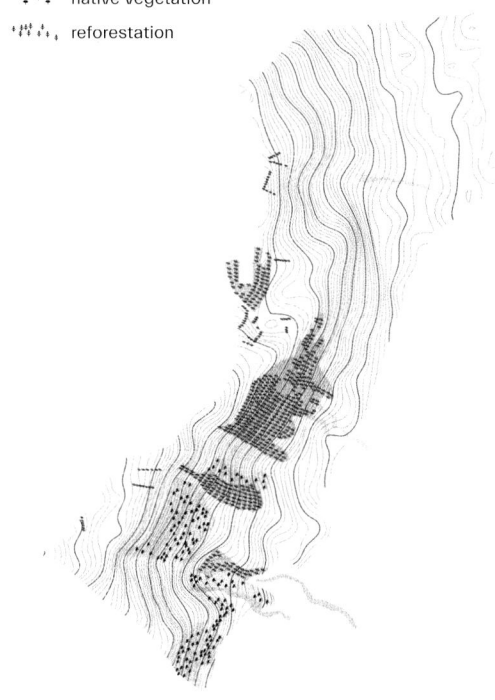

URBANIZATION

▨ points of interest

⋯ urban expansion zone

⌂ street network

TYPOLOGIES

- - - micro-basin

—— natural waterway

⋯⋯ man-made waterway

WORKSHOP #2

URBAN ANDES

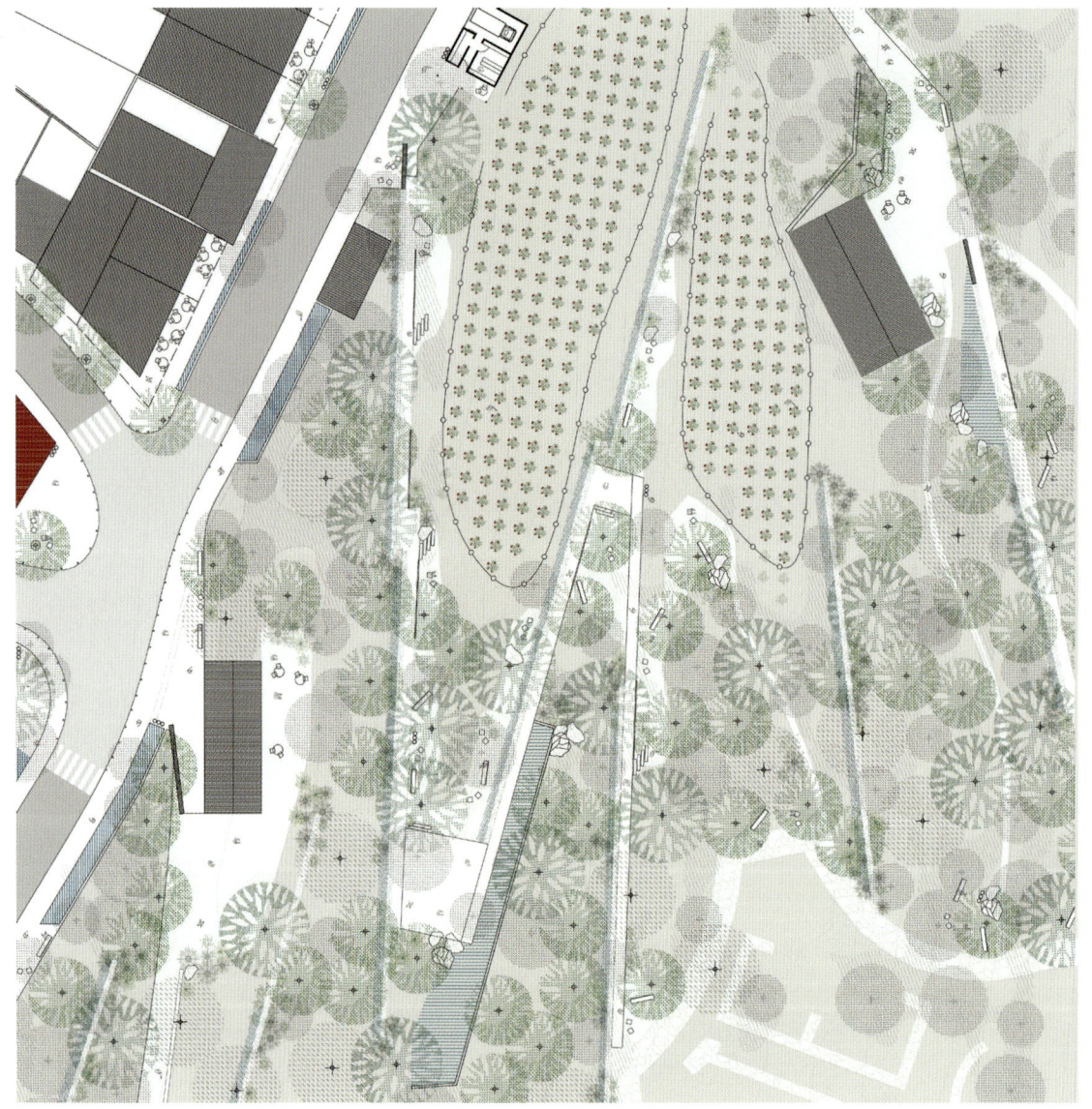

A PRODUCTIVE PARK
An unstable slope near the top of the ridge is reinforced by a series of micro-terraces, pedestrian paths, and small water retention volumes. These divide the terrain into parcels for the production of firewood and lumber, and for the cultivation of fruit, herbs, and *cochinilla*—an insect found on prickly pear cacti with which a crimson dye is made for use in the cosmetic and food industry. By equipping the flank as a productive park, collective use is fostered, and the auto-construction of housing on unsuitable terrain is disincentivized.

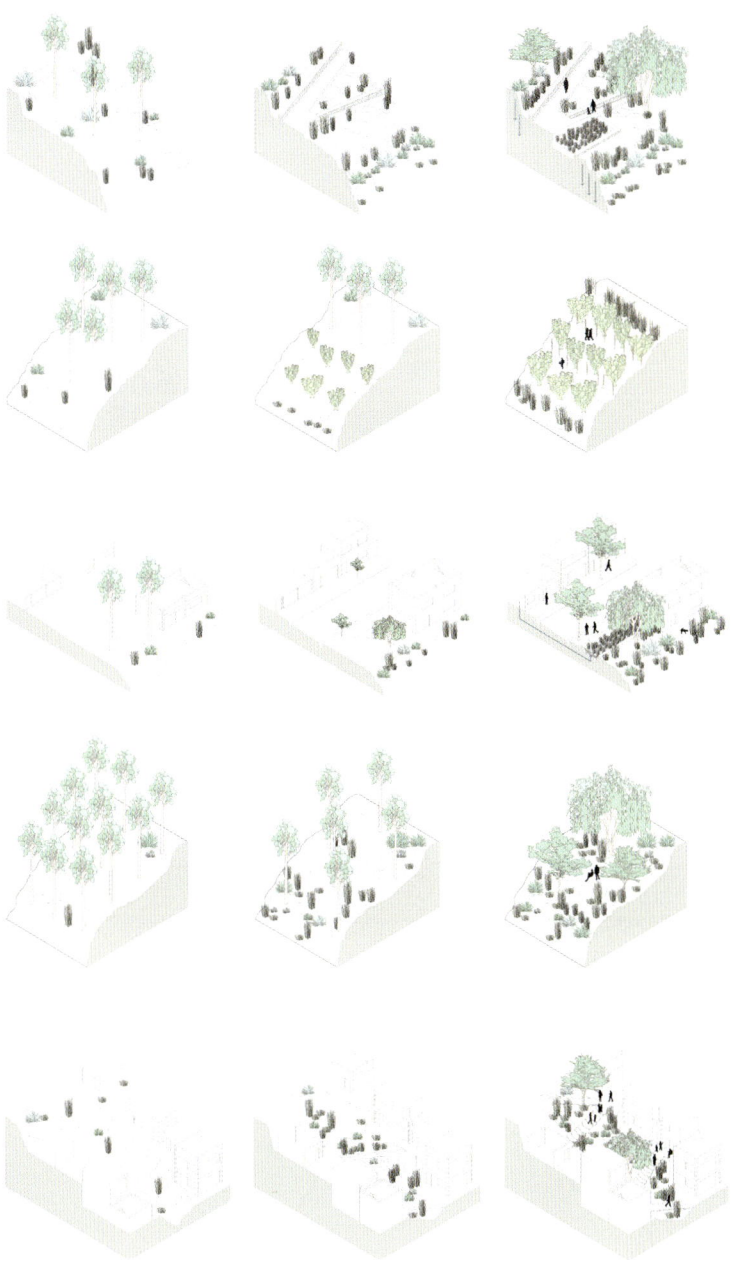

SLOPE CONDITIONS

The short- and long-term transformation of Picota Ridge is further detailed in the context of several representative samples. They present an overview of applicable techniques that lead to future slope conditions: reinforcement of slopes using indigenous vegetation, local retention and infiltration along roads and public squares, and so on. Although not always only site-specific, the trap of the overly generic toolbox is avoided by virtue of having defined these techniques after the actual design work. They are a result of—not a precursor to—the projects.

MOLLEPATA HILL

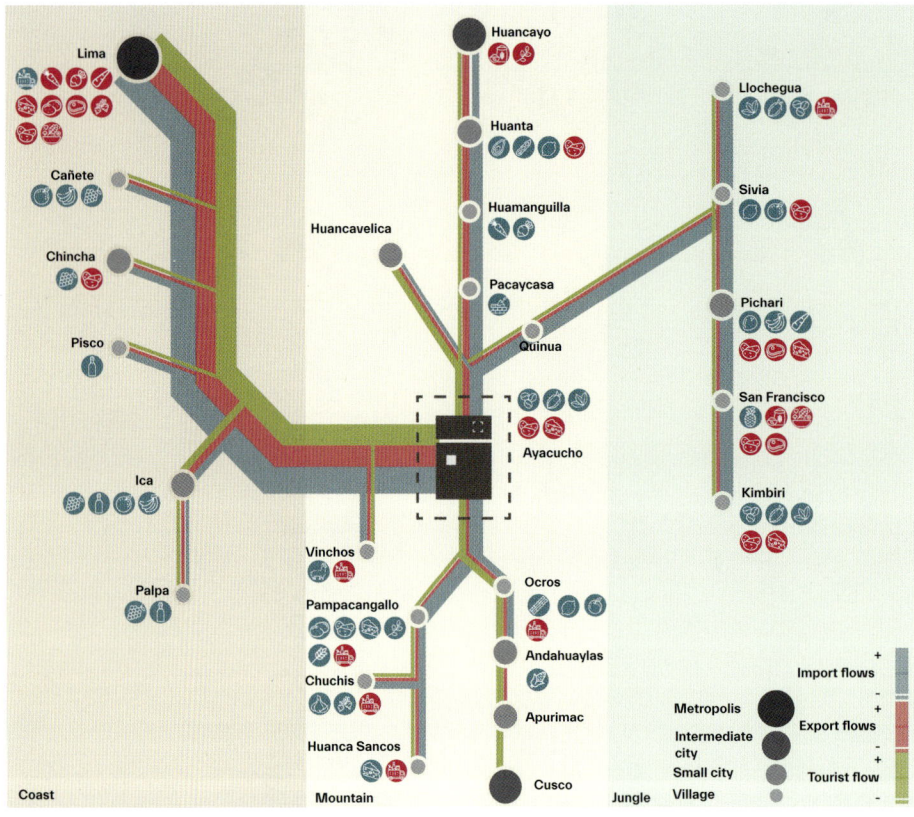

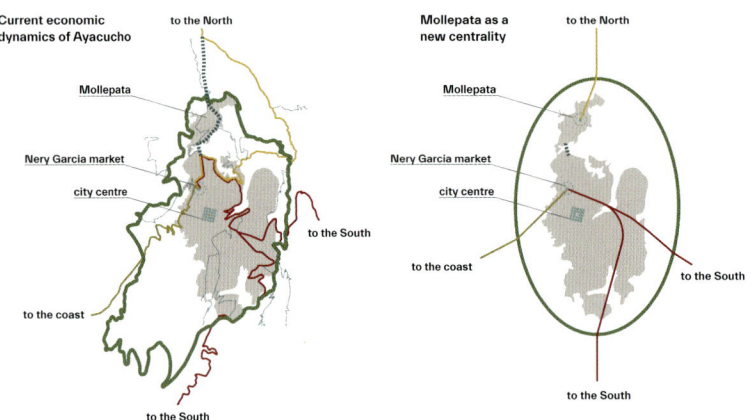

A MARKET ECONOMY

Ayacucho is a key node in a national economic network, connecting the eastern *selva* and *sierra* to Lima. All goods currently flow through the centrally located Nery García Zárate market, which is saturated and a source of traffic congestion. In contrast, the neighbourhood of Mollepata is strategically located at a key access road to the city and houses a population in search of employment and identity. The creation of a new market would bring revenue, activity and pride to a disenfranchised community, while keeping excessive traffic out of the centre.

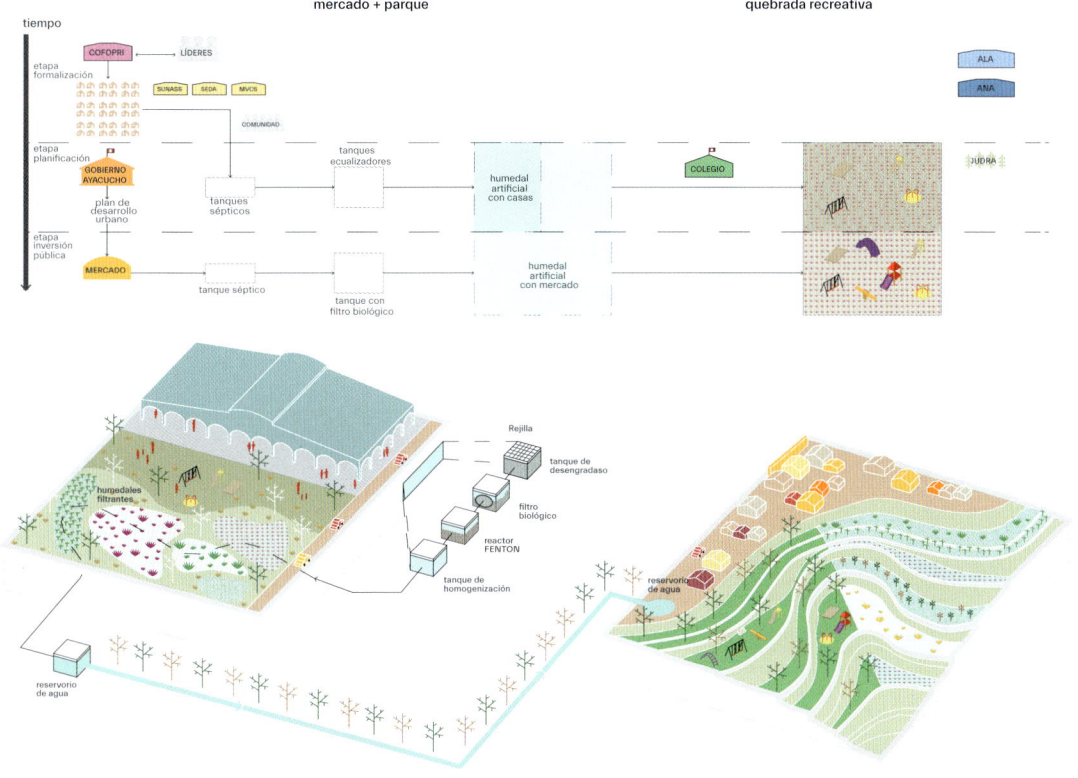

INTERSCALAR WATER NETWORK

The market will feature a water purification system that functions as a catalyst for the creation of an interscalar water network, linking the market with both private water retention tanks and public biofilters. Given the different levels of investment and municipal involvement, it is important that this network can develop simultaneously bottom-up and top-down, in multiple locations and phases, before coagulating into one polycentric whole.

PRODUCTIVE *QUEBRADAS*
Purified waste water expelled from this network is collected along the streets and diverted to the adjacent *quebradas* (dry creek beds). Their steep slopes will be terraced to retain water and topsoil, allowing them to be cultivated by the inhabitants of Mollepata. This new agricultural landscape puts a halt to both erosion and to continued urban expansion. Produce will be primarily for local consumption and can be traded at the market.

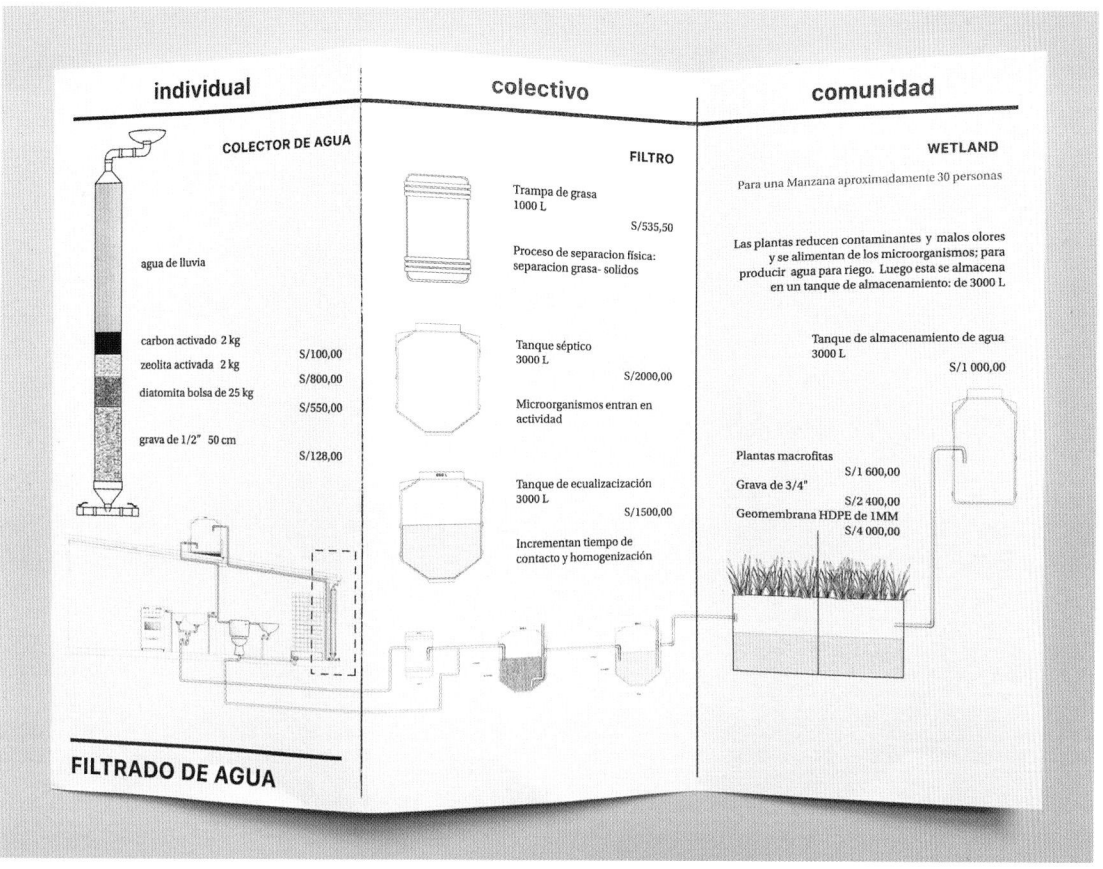

CAPACITY-BUILDING
Within the community itself, building awareness and capacity regarding the value of reusing water is a crucial precondition to the successful establishment and maintenance of this network. Communication tools, such as the brochure shown here, play an important role in explaining what individual households can undertake themselves (and how), and what action must be advocated for on a neighbourhood or municipal scale.

AN ONLINE CONVERSATION

JULY 2020

PARTICIPANTS   VIVIANA D'AURIA   (KU LEUVEN)
                TULIA GARCÍA LEÓN   (CEDAP)
                TAÍCIA MARQUES   (UNALM)
                MARIA ÑOPE   (CCA)
                CARLOS RAMOS ABENSUR   (VORTICE)
                WARD VERBAKEL   (KU LEUVEN)
                BRAM WILLEMS   (CCA)

AN ONLINE CONVERSATION   JULY 2020

Viviana

Looking back at the two years of collaboration in Ayacucho between the different organizations and local partners such as CCA, KU Leuven, CEDAP, the municipality, UNSCH and many others, I wonder if we can identify key moments and major takeaways. In order to take future steps in the resilient transformation of Ayacucho and its broader landscape, we need these identifiers.

Tulia

This is quite broad, but I want to offer some points. Working with CEDAP for a longer period in this area, we were able to establish strategies that we already agree on, like, for example, the protection of natural resources in the highlands. As a learning experience we were able to understand what works and can now find implementation for it elsewhere in more urban contexts. The exchange in that sense came at the right moment in time and space.

The other important aspect is that in order to formulate responses appropriate to the impact of climate change in the Andes, we need to measure the capacity of different technologies implemented in the area. Such scientific interpretation for us has been a very valuable moment.

Bram

From my perspective, as someone who is trying to connect different actors from research and policy around projects, I see our impact as a means to improve resilience and set out pathways towards sustainable development. I found that the workshops' methodology and dynamics are very powerful tools for bringing together different stakeholders and for coming up with designs that visualize possible solutions.

Tulia

For the implementation we need to have any interaction among the actors involved in the whole process, I would point out the collaboration within the team of designers, students, residents, academics, and local experts, and–furthermore– the local decision makers who gradually came to participate in the discussions. They are being fully informed. We are integrating institutional and academic practices, into the minds of younger generations, graduates, students, researchers… That is a sustainable practice in itself.

Bram

Bringing people together to discuss problems or solutions is a different approach. This is not about rocket science: problems can be solved technically and economically, but having these solutions visualized in 3-D space leads to the next question. How do we get there? With what stakeholders? That is for me one of the highest values for this kind of approach. What we still need to achieve, and this is an unresolved task so far, is to translate these design ideas into, for instance, projects that can be undertaken by the municipality.

Maria

An important part of the work was the preparation for stakeholder participation. For months Monica and I prepared the field with meetings, site visits, document collection, and stakeholder mapping, in order understand the interests of various actors and to ensure their participation throughout the process. It contributed a lot to a real compromise on the part of some of the actors, maybe some more than others.

Ward

What has changed between the summer of 2018 and now, in terms of the urban future of Ayacucho and its approach towards water resilience and urban development?

Maria

For example, there is an interest that has been awakened in some actors to work on the concept of urban development linked to water, that is to say, understanding water as a structuring element of the city of Ayacucho. That message, for some actors such as COFOPRI (an entity that works on the formalization of housing ownership rights), has been very important in expanding the conceptual framework that they work in. At the same time it has opened up the possibility for both COFOPRI and the municipality to be able to work together, hand in hand with local actors. This is also framed in a participatory process carried out by the authorities for neighbourhood improvement in areas such as Picota and Mollepata. And there is now more interest from some municipal actors for the management of the historical centre, economic development, as well as planning.

However, the challenge remains in the continuity of the work. Municipal staff change frequently, which means starting the conversation over from the beginning, explaining the strategy, goals, and concepts. That is something very real that influences the quality of the work we do and interferes with the expectations of results that we want to achieve.

Taícia

The municipality of Ayacucho has been developing a Sustainable Urban Mobility Plan, which was interrupted by the pandemic, and an Integral Plan for Traffic Management, lacking an overall vision. Additionally, with the support of the Ministry of Housing, Construction, and Sanitation, they are also developing the regional plan for Huamanga and revising the urban development plan for Ayacucho. From what I see, those plans are still under construction and could benefit from our reading of the region, with urban micro-basins, for example. Does the participatory process with the local actors we have met support the development of these plans, learning from the workshops as we imagine it? I would add that another challenge is multi-sector work. The drainage plan for the historic centre, for example, is already installed but does not include all those strategies that were designed during the workshops. How do we get these actors, who were involved in the design process, heard at a governmental level? Involving the population is still very important, but we have to have strategies in both directions, bottom-up and top-down.

Ward

Up and down, but also multi-sectoral. We need to start addressing such complex systems and challenges in a multi-sectoral way. Especially if the means and capacities of the people are scarce. Can we see first signs of such cross-expertise and integrated approaches here in Ayacucho?

Taícia

I think this is key, to have a more holistic plan, to understand this city as a system that will deal with the water as much as with everything else. So, you need to talk with these many secretaries, stakeholders, and sectors during the workshops. The thing is, how do we get them to work together? How do we see that if I am working on the mobility question, that work will impact water drainage and ecology too? So how can they join forces and move forward on these challenges?

Ward

We should remain very optimistic, in the sense that–by having organised such exchanges and bringing people together to the discussion, especially young people that are in education and training–there really is a dissemination of ideas, and people do start to see things in certain ways. This can trickle down into actual change on the ground. It is a slow process, but it is probably a more resilient process than looking for one quick fix.

Bram

The municipality of Ayacucho has five separate districts that make up the urban area, with separate administrators. I would say that strategies have to focus on working with neighbourhood organizations so that they become the drivers that continue bringing these ideas to the attention of the municipalities. That is needed if we want to make some impact, using all this work by academics and engineers. There has been a lot of work done, and we don't want to just end with a nice book.

Carlos

Complementing that, unfortunately, the political and governmental reality in our country is quite unstable, and that often brings down many positive initiatives like the one we are seeing now. My advice is to maintain a certain independence from the internal government administration, because many times it is too cumbersome, and sometimes it even serves very different interests.

Viviana

How do local constituencies and organizations benefit from such research and exchange? How is the knowledge used? Where has it been applied?

Maria

In two follow-up sessions after the workshop, conducted in Quechua and Spanish, we noticed an interest from the leaders of Mollepata for collective action. It was a good method for transmitting information and concepts of the research in their own language.

They were very interested in building the wetlands as a way to collect rainwater and treat wastewater, integrated into the urban design, both on small private plots and on communal lands. Whether they realize these with their own finances or with the support of the municipality, that was not so much the issue; they were more concerned with making a collective decision and realizing a small pilot project.

Another thing achieved after the workshop is that the economic development director asked us to develop a wetland at one of the schools in the city of Ayacucho. The objective of the wetland, obviously, is to treat wastewater, but that the treated wastewater also can be used to irrigate green areas and decrease the use of drinking water. Furthermore, we worked with one of the participants, Russell, on a water information centre at the Cuchoquesera Dam for Sunass (the drinking water regulator in Peru). He has remained active in Ayacucho, working on initiatives and the dissemination of knowledge.

We have also participated in the Youth Water Forum, in September 2019, where the results of the first workshop were shared. This drew a lot of attention to other young people and organizations that work with water. Especially the broader view that water is not only a matter of open areas in the highlands, but also to see the urban development on water-based principles, as well as how it is articulated with the idea of where we want to live, and how we want to live.

Bram

That goes to show that our challenges are universal, though the solutions depend on the specific context. Often, when one lives in one place, you don't notice many details that an outsider can.

As long as we don't start from the perspective of 'we come to solve your problems'. Rather we come to learn together and to see how our contribution can help you solve problems and have a dialogue between interests.

I think the experience of Urban Andes has been quite successful, because it has a long-term strategy. Several projects have contributed, as well as the presence of a strong motivated local team.

Carlos

In countries such as Peru, urban expansion is much more informal than in other Latin American countries. Within that informality there are urban settlements in process of consolidation in risk zones, which can go hand in hand with this type of intervention. This relates to the deep roots of ancestral/cultural baggage: the cultural value is quite strong, and that you can tap into for urban processes as well. A vision may include the water system and the management of the natural resource, but it should also identify the sociocultural factor and the ancestral heritage, which is quite strong in Ayacucho.

Maria

In order to make an intervention more assertive or successful–related to what Carlos pointed out about knowing the local reality–I think that something important we have done is to constantly deal with problems of management and the different visions that we have regarding how we approach something. And this is valuable.

When I left Lima, I found myself in Ayacucho, interacting with people from different regions, from different places. A very important subject was the subject of gender, for example. I had meetings only with men, most of the time; they were all managers, officials, or technicians. Ayacuchan women, professionals, almost always maintained an unequal relationship vis-à-vis other decision makers. On the contrary, my relationship was always more horizontal with those women, which generated a lot of trust as well. Monica, representing an international perspective (Ecuador, Belgium), opened other conversations. How are they working with the water issue in Ecuador? Would it be possible to do internships with the water company there? I think that you can generate very interesting cooperation between institutions (more centralized in Lima, such as the CCA) and local organizations.

Tulia

This reminds us of several things. What I have valued quite a bit during this experience is that between collaborators we managed to have a very participatory method. The strategy of being in the field executing projects, and the continued dialogue with broader partners, allowed continuous monitoring and evaluation, as well as gradual incorporation of lessons learned.

Viviana

Reciprocity is a constant although ever-evolving practice in the Andes. Do you feel it could be further supported to address the challenges of water management through community-built infrastructures? What can the concept of urban *faena* today teach us when rethinking urban water systems? What forms of support would be required to complement *faenas* as a means to reconfigure contemporary urban design and planning?

Tulia

Reciprocity has been an ancestral practice in Peru, but I believe that more than a tradition it is a social form of work that exists between High Andean communities, families, or indigenous communities. It is a way of optimizing labour force and resources for one common goal. It is a thread that brings families and communities together, allowing decision makers to act with greater emphasis.

The question is whether the challenges of water management through infrastructure built by the community can take place. In Ayacucho, a very successful experience took place, which has been recognized by the government through the Ministry of the Environment. Communities building micro-dykes, for instance–for damming water, irrigating, and replenishing the groundwater table– has been incorporated as a national policy–not only a regional, local one, but also national.

Carlos

Participatory work in cities is growing in strength in Latin America, maybe because of the high degree of informality in our urban form. Expansion in Latin

America manifests itself physically before the structured urban system is planned. Therefore, there is a practice of adaptation plans, following sometimes illogical settlement behaviours into risk zones.

If participatory work is carried out with commitment to the population, along with the appropriate tools and social dynamics, appropriation can take place. An agreement could be signed in order to carry out part of this post-intervention themselves, with the workforce of the residents. A great way to also help communities take shape–in areas that often emerge as new neighbourhoods and land grabbing–through the organization of such reciprocal work. The tool of *mapa parlante*, for example, serves for gathering information within such emerging social structures and for prioritizing what type of interventions the neighbourhood really needs.

Ward

The technique of *mapa parlante*–as we encountered it during our visit to the headwater communities, explaining in a graphical way how they plan the use and crop rotation of their land–is an example that really struck us, since it is a tool that local communities and urban designers and planners share. The importance of developing shared knowledge is a successful example in this Andean context. How could a more widespread 'Andean practice' emerge from these practices, and which main features would it have?

Tulia

In the day-to-day practice of the communities, this practice not only serves to identify a current state of a territory, but also to make medium- and long-term projections. The *mapas parlantes* are not only an instrument for peasant communities but also for urban areas. We use it in education as well (primary, secondary, and university level) to project their vision of the future.

It is a powerful way to reflect on the current state of location of all their natural resources–water; the characteristics of their soils; water sources; suitable areas of afforestation, or those that are afforested; areas specifically for grazing; wetlands–and the services (education, drinking water...) and those that they do not have; they are located on the maps for future projection. They voice their demands towards their local government regarding the decision about participatory budgeting.

So, I think the *mapas parlantes* have been seen throughout the whole process used here. The projections in Mollepata and Picota during the workshop, for example, quickly were picked up by the communities. And that convinces sectors and organizations, decision makers, to define priorities and then implement them.

Taícia

The use of *mapas parlantes* may be adapted to different scales of action, working with peasants, working with urban areas, but what I see is a potential for information exchange between those living in urban areas and those living in rural areas. We are quite accustomed to thinking about a city and a rural area as two isolated entities. I think that this exchange of information, putting in practice the *mapa parlante* with the people that live in lower and higher parts of the basin –it could be a way of understanding all the problems.

In this case of water (and it can also be food), there is the dependence that we have from the city to those much larger areas as well. How the city can act reducing this dependency, or what resources are available for much longer and with better quality, would be an interesting contribution, to exchange a little more between these two territorial sectors.

Viviana

The Alameda River that crosses Ayacucho's centre can be much more than an infrastructure of control for seasonal floods. Its transformation from a walled flushing canal and waste collector into a significant public space structure for the densely populated central areas is much needed.

Maria

The Alameda River has great potential–and great importance locally. It is the largest river that crosses the city of Ayacucho; the residual water from the sewage treatment plant of the city is discharged into that river; people use it for washing clothes, bathing, recreation, small scale agriculture... There is even a shelter for rescued animals, a zoo on the river bank. We can speak of the Alameda River as a floodable park. To go from seeing only the river as a river, rather seeing the river as integrated and in harmony with the environment. Those ideas from the workshops attracted a lot of attention with the local actors in Ayacucho. Parks that also could be green areas to help risk management in Picota generated a lot of enthusiasm, a lot of interest. This is something that could be applied to the Alameda River as well.

The Alameda River also separates people who are on the other bank (much poorer, more marginalized in some cases, those who witnessed violence of the internal armed conflict of social violence in Peru). Those who live across the river versus those who reside in the more dynamic and central area of the city. The river can expand the spaces of culture, meeting, memory, fraternity towards the other bank; it could be done very easily in the Alameda; it has great potential to work these things out.

Carlos

I think this is the most difficult question. How to revitalize the river? After analyzing the subject and looking for references on the national level, almost all the cities of Peru–from the Andes or the coast– do not face the river. In this sense, probably, the emphasis should be put on the use of complementary equipment in order to activate the use of the river as a public space.

Taícia

I think that is a very important point, the systematic view of the valley which receives several channels, the dry beds, tributaries...

I think that to manage the area downstream, first, we need to buffer the impact of the waters that come from the basin. Probably, the volume of the water and the speed of the water have increased at certain points and diminished drastically at others. Climate change and its impact on the water system, being extremely complex, needs to be evaluated before changing anything in the river.